DR. · LLOYD · JOHN
OGILVIE

FREEDOM IN THE SPIRIT

*Experiencing the Release
of God's Power in Your Life*

HARVEST HOUSE PUBLISHERS
Eugene, Oregon 97402

FREEDOM IN THE SPIRIT

Copyright © 1984 by Harvest House Publishers
Eugene, Oregon 97402

Library of Congress Catalog Card Number 83-82318
ISBN 0-89081-400-7

Printed in the United States of America.

Table of Contents

Introduction

We all feel it. The longing to be free. Truly free. Free to be and express our real selves. Free to enjoy life, ourselves, others. Free to receive and give love, forgiveness, acceptance. Free to pull out all the stops and live with boldness and courage.

And yet, so often we are tied down by feelings of guilt; bound by frustrating anxieties; uptight over needing people's approval; incarcerated by their criticisms or negative opinions; and locked up in fears about the future. We spend so much of our lives in the restrictive prisons of our own or others' reservations. We yearn to break free and live.

The startling thing is that many Christians do not feel any more free than those who make no pretense of having faith. Years of hearing the gospel and the liberating truths of the Lord's love, justification through the cross, and unqualified grace have not released many believers from the syndrome of insecurity, self-justification, and fear of failure. Why is this?

That question has been troubling me for years. I have asked it about myself, about church members

5

throughout the nation, and the thousands of viewers who write me each week about their deepest needs and urgent questions in response to my church's national television ministry. Listening to people has brought me to an alarming conclusion: Most people do not feel free to live life with delight and joy. Instead, their years are blighted with self-doubt, caution, and fear.

This conclusion led me to begin a prolonged study of what it means to be truly free. I did an in-depth study of the key passages of the Bible about authentic freedom. At the same time, I sought to be ruthlessly honest with myself in thinking through my own pilgrimage in becoming a progressively free person in Christ. Then in the quiet of profound prayer and Spirit-guided reflection, I confronted areas in my life where I still felt unfree. How could the Lord set me free more fully?

In addition to my biblical study of how Christ set people free during His incarnation and in His post-resurrection, post-Pentecost ministry, I studied the lives of people through history who had known joyous liberation. Then from thirty years of ministry, I collected the stories of people I have known personally who have been unshackled by Christ. Finally, to make my investigation precise for today, I asked my congregation and the viewers of our television program to write and tell me the areas in their lives where they needed Christ to set them free. All of this study concerning the meaning of true freedom became the basis of the conclusions I share with you in this book.

My central purpose is to communicate what I've discovered about how to think about freedom and how to feel free. My thrust is that emotions follow thought; what we feel has first been in our thinking. Confused, fearful thoughts cause constricted, unfree feelings. But the good news is that Christ can change our thinking and release our feelings. He promised that we can know the truth and the truth will set us free. But how does that happen?

I believe the explanations and illustrations of this book will help you discover the major causes of our lack of freedom and *how a fresh experience of the status, the security, and the strength we have in Christ can open the prison doors that keep us locked up in self-negation, inhibition, and tenseness.*

I seek to be both practical and personal in showing how to receive healing of debilitating memories, how to forgive ourselves and others, how to recover the feeling of freedom when we've lost it, how to change from being a people-pleaser to a people-affirmer, how to be free to release others to live at full potential, how to become a riverbed for the inflow and outflow of the all-sufficient Spirit of the Lord, how to live care-freely in the midst of problems and difficulties, overcoming worry and fear, and how to enjoy and laugh at ourselves when we become grim and uptight. Christ the liberator, through the indwelling power of His Spirit, is ready and able to unbind us and free us to soar.

Each chapter is based on one or more of the key biblical passages about freedom in the Spirit. These passages contain the truth that reorients our thinking about the Lord's grace. The application of these truths is illustrated by the stories of real people today who are experiencing new freedom in the Spirit.

Throughout the book I try to grapple honestly with

the contemporary struggles and freedom-sapping anxieties we all face. In a realistic, down-to-earth, and personal way, I feel compelled to put in writing the secrets the Lord has revealed of how to realize, feel, and express our "rebirth-right" of freedom in Christ. Thinking this through has brought me to a greater freedom than I've ever known. My prayer is that reading about this unfolding adventure in freedom will be as liberating to you as it has been to me.

This book has been written in direct response to people's expression of their longings to be free. Therefore, there is a real dialogue throughout the book. Many of the thoughts and discoveries I share with you as I write have been in messages to my beloved congregation. The responses of church members to those messages have sharpened and refined many insights as I listened and talked with those who came with questions and comments.

This ongoing dialogue is a constant reminder to communicate what I speak and write in deeply personal terms—to deal with real-life concerns. Added to this dialogue, the correspondence with the television audience I mentioned earlier keeps me in touch with what people all across the country are thinking and feeling. My hope is that this book will be a continuation of that conversation—a dialogue between you and me.

I am also gratified by the people who make possible the completion of a book like this: Robert Hawkins, Sr., President of Harvest House, has been a very encouraging friend from the inception on through the development of the book; my administrative assistant, Jerlyn Gonzalez, has been a faithful fellow worker in overseeing the preparation of the manuscript for publication; Georgiana Walker's skills as editor maximized the effort; and Christina Hemme typed the manuscript through several retypings.

Now let's press on to discover the secret of freedom in the Spirit!

—LLOYD JOHN OGILVIE

1

How Are You Thinking Today?

Chapter One

How Are You Thinking Today?

f I were to ask you the question, "Are you free?" your immediate response would probably be, "Free? Why, of course, I'm an American and live in a free country. I can do, say, believe what I want to!"

How Free?

But if I were to ask the same question in a slightly different way, it is likely your response would not be as quick or definite. If I asked, "Are you a free person?" many of you would respond, "I'm not so sure about that. Often I am tense, fret about things, and am frustrated by people and situations."

Then, if I were to press you further with the even more personal question, "Do you *feel* really free?" chances are your response would be even less positive. If you are like many people with whom I talk about their experiences of freedom on a feeling level, you would say honestly and frankly, "No, so often I don't feel free. I don't feel released to be myself, love myself or others spontaneously, and respond to life with gusto and without fear. Often I feel bound up, boxed in, cautious, frustrated. The attitudes and negativism of people can rob me of feeling free. When I don't measure up and get down on myself I don't feel free.

"Yesterday's failures sometimes make me feel I have no right to be free to enjoy myself today. Or when I feel pressured by people or demanding schedules, I feel anything but free. I get uptight when I feel inadequate or insecure. Sometimes I am so worried about things, I get a churning feeling of dread. Feel free? Well, far too little of the time!"

Ever feel that way? Of course, we all have.

Listening to people's responses to questions concerning freedom has brought me to an alarming conclusion: Millions of politically free Americans do not feel free. We live in the land of liberty, but many of us feel imprisoned spiritually and emotionally.

What is Freedom?

Personal freedom is an emancipated, fearless condition of our minds which is expressed in our personalities and in our feelings about ourselves, others, life's challenges and opportunities, and our expectations for what the future holds. Using that definition of freedom, most people would say that they are not free.

The distressing thing is that many of us who call ourselves Christians are as uptight and unfree as those who make no pretense of believing in Christ who came, and comes, to set us free. In spite of our confession of Him as Savior and Lord, we deny our-

selves our "rebirth-right" of enjoying Him and ourselves. Feelings of guilt, defensiveness, anxiety, self-
justification, and perfectionism lock us up in a prison
of our own making.

We quote the salient verses of the Bible about
freedom, and yet very few of us feel free. We try
to live on our own strength and run out of steam.
Past failures incarcerate us in self-incrimination; fear
of failing in the future immobilizes us and makes us
cautious. We surrender our worth to other people's
opinions and negative criticism. Our struggle with
the stress of being adequate exhausts us. Efforts at
self-induced perfectionism spill over in impatience
with ourselves, and eventually, with others. We get
angry at ourselves and become critical of others.

You know what I mean. Think of those days when
you wake up not feeling free to be yourself, not
delighted in the person you are, and not able to shake
the negative impact of what people have said or done
to you. And if you are like most, those feelings
become a habit. They become more familiar than a
carefree, liberated feeling of joyous freedom.

Worry becomes a conditioned response to life. We
expect the worst and it usually happens. Concerns
engulf us. Pressures mount. People disappoint or hurt
us. Obligations and responsibilities often are handled
with grim determination. Our self-imposed sentence
is: We have no right to feel free with things the way
they are.

My deep concern over this no-right-to-feel-free attitude led me to a prolonged study of freedom. In
order to make my research precise in how people
feel about their freedom or lack of it, I asked my congregation and our national television audience to
share with me areas in which they needed to be free.

A card was provided on which people could complete the sentence, "I need to be set free in:_____." Some of the responses were capsulized in one word. Others wrote sentences of more complete explanation. Allow me to share a sampling of people's longing to be free.

Anxiety, worry, fear, guilt, and insecurity topped the list of thousands of responses. For example, one person wrote, "A gnawing sense of anxiety about the future. For years I've heard and thought I believed Romans 8:28—'That all things work together for good to those who love God, to those who are called according to His purpose.' And yet, during the past couple of years, my trust has been shaken. How do I get free of this uneasiness?"

Another person expressed the longing to be free of worry. "I trust my problems to the Lord and then snatch them back and try to handle them myself as if I had never committed them to Him. Why do I do this?" The same concern was shared by another who asked, "Why can't I overcome the anguish of worry over my family and friends? I pray, surrendering them to the Lord before I go to sleep at night and then wake up after a few hours of sleep and worry on through the night. I imagine the worst and go over things in my mind picturing all the terrible things which might happen. How can I get free of this worry?"

One person sounded the alarm of worry over money, a concern expressed by hundreds of others. "I worry over money—having enough and keeping what little I have. The cost of living goes up and so does my stress over money." This need to be free of money worries was expressed by both those who were facing financial crises and those who were troubled about the fact that anxiety continued even after they had become more secure financially.

I was amazed by how many people utilized the opportunity of making an anonymous response to talk about their yearning to be free of guilt. One wrote, "I need to be set free of the guilt I feel over some failures and sins years ago. I am told the Lord forgives me, but I keep on remembering. Guess I can't...or won't...forgive myself." Another person put the same need in another way. "At the end of most every day I think back over what I've said and done. I feel guilty about both what I shouldn't have done and what I wish I had done. I'm tired of not measuring up!" And a father wrote remorsefully, "My kids are grown. I see their faults and realize all that I should have done differently in raising them. I wish I had been a stronger father, given my kids a sharper edge to cut on. What do I do now? Guilt keeps me tied up in knots." The causes of guilt expressed by so many others were varied, enumerating the things we all feel. The question beneath all of them, however, was how to get free of the prison of guilt.

And fears that keep us from being free? The responses were as varied as those who wrote about guilt. One of the greatest fears, underneath all the others expressed, was the fear of failure. A man put it flatly, "I've had successes and failures. My problem is that I forget the good things and remember the failures. Thinking too much about them has made me repeat the same mistakes. How can I get free of this panic about failing?"

Running a close second to this first group of responses, was the group which expressed a longing to be free of negative attitudes, opinions, and judgments. In this category were the people who were suffering from other peoples' negativism and also those who realized that they needed to be freed from being inordinately negative. A woman wrote, "People pull me down. It's almost impossible to be a positive person with all the negativism around me." And a man put it this way, "I used to be a very positive, affirming person. Some disappointments lately have made me less than hopeful. How can I get free of the discouragement I feel about people?"

The same concern, expressed pointedly, came from another person who was feeling uptight. "I've drifted into being down on people. I guess I know my own mixed motives and question theirs." The deeper cause of negativism was articulated by a further response. "I've given up the luxury of faith in God's timely interventions. I pray and nothing seems to happen. People talk about miracles, healings, and answers to prayer. Maybe I'm doing something wrong, but I really wonder if God does care or is involved in our daily problems. I'd like to be free of that doubt."

We all face times of discouragement. It builds a prison with seemingly immovable bars. The problem is that we get into the habit of negative thinking and find it difficult to break out of the incarceration it imposes. That was vividly confessed by another respondent to my question about freedom. He said, "I guess I've been given the questionable talent of discernment. I size people up quickly and can see their faults and inadequacies immediately. I'm usually right, but wish I had more faith in God to change them. I need to be freed to believe more in His power to change personality."

The most urgent of the responses from people battling with negativism came from a person who confessed, "I need Christ to set me free from being so negative about myself—it's ruining my attitudes at home and at work. People tell me I've become a cynic. That has shocked me. How does Christ help a person like me?"

The third largest category of responses came from people who needed to be set free in their relationships—freedom to be themselves, express love and forgiveness, encouragement and affirmation to others. Many in this group desired freedom from needing people's approval so much that they were losing a sense of their own value and self-esteem. One person wrote, "I realize how much I need people's approval. Criticism really throws me into a tailspin. I'd like to be set free of that." Another said, "Christ needs to set me free of being a people-pleaser! I'm like putty in people's hands. I need affirmation so much, I keep doing and saying things people will applaud rather than being myself."

A church leader wrote, "When someone levels a blast of criticism or questions my actions or beliefs, I get into a grim mood. It takes me days, sometimes weeks, to recapture my security in Christ. I wish I could be so free that it wouldn't take so long to battle back to the assurance that I'm loved and forgiven by the Lord." A successful pastor wrote somewhat the same concern in a personal note in response to my question about his need for freedom in Christ. "Lloyd, I get hundreds of affirmations and one unfair criticism and all I remember is the one crank. On your television program you asked us to write sharing where we need Christ to set us free. Well, for what it's worth, that's mine!"

This third group also contained the expressions of need of those who desired to become free to become channels of love and affirmation to others. A woman captured the feelings of hundreds of others when she wrote, "I need Christ to set me free to say the loving things I feel but often neglect expressing."

Also, a large proportion of the responses about freedom in relationships articulated sadness over broken relationships in which misunderstandings and hurts had strained and then snapped the bond of love and friendship. A man shared his ache about that. "I need Christ to set me free of my righteous indignation. I feel I'm right, but that hasn't healed the breakdown in communication. I can't set aside my values just to affect a reconciliation. And yet, the strained relationship is keeping me unfree!"

This man's dilemma was stated by so many others who were caught in the bind of resentment. "When people do something wrong," one person wrote, "I can't set aside my belief in right and wrong, God's law, and what He expects. I feel someone has to hold the line. When is forgiveness simply sloppy sentimentalism, approval of what's wrong?" And a less severe, but no less troubled reply voicing the same problem, "I know I should forgive and then accept people. I say the words, but the wrong keeps coming back to my mind."

The fourth largest group contained the desire of people for freedom from debilitating memories that limit freedom in the present. Hundreds of people simply wrote their need in four pointed words: the healing of memories. One who elaborated explained in this way, "I need Christ to set me free of hurting memories of the past—to remember to forget!"

The next group contained the stresses of life which

keep people from a sense of being free: pressures, demands, lack of time, changes, and physical illnesses. A woman said, "I long to be free of stress. My life is like a pressure cooker. My blood is boiling with agitation most of the time. I read all that's written about the debilitating power of inordinate stress for our health and ask for Christ's help in handling times when I get an overload on the circuits of my life. I want to get free of living in constant stress."

The final group of responses listed out the compulsive habits which limit freedom and hold people captive. Among these were not only the hope of liberation from addictions of various kinds, but also from habit patterns of personality and uncreative responses to life.

Most of the people who responded were Christians. The opportunity to express the causes of their not feeling free brought a ready response. It was as if people said, "Thank you for asking. I want to be free and here's where I'm feeling imprisoned. Help!"

The fascinating thing is that the self-evaluations were all based on some personal standard. Most Christians have a vision of what a free person in Christ should be. But at the same time, they are aware of an engulfing sense of not being free.

Think Freedom, Feel Freely

What I have suspected for a long time was confirmed. True spiritual freedom is rooted in God's unassailable truth which controls our thinking brain and pervades our emotions. When we do not feel free it is usually because of emotions which have not been brought under control of our thinking. An emotion of fear, anxiety, worry, or insecurity is rooted to some distorted thought about who we are in our relationship to the Lord.

So often when we meet another person we ask, "How are you feeling today?" or "How are you?" Instead, we should ask, "How are you thinking?" or "How's your thinking today?" How we feel is directly traceable to what we think about what has happened to us or around us. So much of our thinking is not controlled and conditioned by the Lord—what He has done for us, and His unconditional love for us. Becoming a truly free person requires battling for truth in the midst of the untruth of our irrational thinking which creates our incarcerated, unfree feelings.

Emotions follow thought. We cannot change how we feel until we change our thinking. Solomon was right, "For as he thinks in his heart, so is he..." (Proverbs 23:7). Our perception of life will control how we feel about it in any one day. Circumstances do not control our feelings. What we think about those circumstances results in our feelings of joy or frustration. Often we feel victimized by our emotional responses to people. But, in between the impact of what they say or do that distresses us, is the split second cognitive response that triggers our feelings. Often, what we think is based on ideas and accumulated attitudes creased in the memory factors of our thinking brain which are not consistent with Christ, the gospel, and His revealed truth.

Christ our liberator stated clearly the basis of our freedom in John 8:31-36. It is His emancipation proclamation. From it we learn the vital importance of thought as the basis of feeling freedom. A careful exposition of the entire passage becomes the authoritative, biblical foundation of our "think freedom, feel freely" thesis. Jesus said, "If you abide in My word, you are My disciples indeed. And you shall know the truth, and the truth shall make you free" (John 8:31,32).

Note the progression. We are to continue to abide. *Meinēte,* from *menō,* to abide, implies consistent, continuing abiding. We are to dwell in Christ's word and allow that word to dwell in us. That means what Christ has said is to be the basis of all that we think about God, life, ourselves, people, the future, death, and eternal security.

Abiding in Christ's words fills us with His truth. The word truth here as He uses it means absolute reality. His clear, messianic assertion is the basis of our convictions. "I am the truth," He said with divine authority. He is God with us revealing the true nature of God and man. What He said, did, and proclaimed must become the objective standard of our beliefs, convictions, attitudes, and reactions. Bringing all thought captive to Him who is sublime truth is the source of liberated emotions.

All that we feel that makes us unfree is tied to some thought inconsistent with Christ's truth. He promises that we shall know the truth and that truth will make us free. I believe He means intellectual, spiritual, and emotional freedom. The Greek word for freedom used in this liberating promise is *eleutherōsei,* the future active indicative of *eleutheroō.* The future is used because at this time in His ministry, Jesus looked forward to the completed work of salvation He came to accomplish. And so, looking back, we contemplate the truth which sets us free in the context of the cross, the resurrection, and the infilling of His Spirit through Pentecost.

Foundation for Freedom

What Jesus said becomes the foundation, the basis of our status, our security, and our strength. Feelings of lack of freedom usually are caused by a denial in our thinking of one or all three of these crucial gifts. Our feelings of guilt, insecurity, and worrisome anxiety are all caused by incomplete linkage between claiming the status, security, and strength of the Savior. Let's consider these three aspects of the truth that sets us free and see how they are worked out in our daily emotional responses.

Our status. The truth of Christ establishes our status. He is the unmerited love of God incarnate. His love is given before we can earn or deserve it. We are forgiven in spite of what we say or do. Christ who said repeatedly, "Neither do I condemn you; go in peace," went to the cross to suffer and die for the forgiveness of our sins.

A Christ-centered, cross-oriented mind is one that is rooted in convictions of justification, forgiveness, and eternal acceptance. Christ sublimely changes our minds about self-justification, self-oblation, and self-condemnation.

Just as surely as Copernicus changed the world's perception of the flatness of the planet earth; or Newton asserted gravitation; or Einstein established the theory of relativity; Christ radically transformed our understanding of true freedom. To fly in the face of the truth these benchmark scientists gave us about the natural world would be absurd and foolhardy. Much more so, when we think contrary to Christ's atonement of our sins and His complete and eternal justification for us, we trigger emotions which eventually rob us of the freedom He died to give us.

And yet, think of all the days you have spent feeling unfree because of guilt and subsequent self-justification. Remember all those down times when your feelings were pervaded by self-condemnation because of mistakes in the past or fear of failure in the future? Or remember how often you have felt unfree when you based your perceptions of your value and worth on other people's opinions and were dragged into the prison of feeling their judgments or negative evaluations? Consider how much of life has been spent nursing feelings of hurt over the rejections and put-downs of people. You did not feel free as a result. You probably became cautious and reserved in the expression of your own unique personality.

In each time of emotional lack of freedom, liberation comes only through clear thinking about our status as the chosen, called, cherished, forgiven, and accepted loved ones of the Lord. We need to wake up to reality, see our irrationality, and ask the Lord to help us live His truth in totality.

Our security. That leads us to consider the assurance of our security. So many of the irrational thoughts which trigger our feelings of bondage come as a result of thinking we are alone. But just as our status is established by claiming we are Christ's possession, our security is engendered by His presence. Fear and worry flourish in our feelings when we think that we must face life alone.

The truth which sets us free is not only Christ's atoning death, but His resurrection victory. Death is defeated and our fear of dying is overcome by the truth that we belong to Him for eternity. All lesser fears, mysteriously rooted to this one great fear of non-existence, are defeated and drained of their power.

When life piles in on us and we face its responsibilities, we must think our way through the maze of feelings of inadequacy to the triumphant truth that we belong to a victorious Savior who won—and wins. The resurrection asserts the reliability of our intervening Lord who invades our difficulties and gives us the courage we need. Thinking clearly about our Savior's resurrection releases feelings of freedom for the future. Our Savior promises, "Lo, I am with you always..." (Matthew 28:20).

Christ's strength. Now press on to the third basis of our freedom. Christ's strength. Not only the status of His possession, the security of His presence, but the strength of His power transforms our thinking and subsequently our feelings of being free. We can be free to face the challenges of life only if we are sure that Christ Himself will be the power to give us exactly what we need in each situation. He promised that He would be with us and in us. That's the secret of thinking freedom. His indwelling Spirit is the Spirit of truth. It is important to remember that when Jesus promised the Holy Spirit, He coupled that with the promise of His own return to be with us forever. We are to abide in Him and He in us.

Freedom comes as a result of a habitual pattern of thinking His truth, and claiming His power every day. He gives power to think His thoughts and will to do His will. He floods our emotions with the fruit of His Spirit—love, joy, peace, patience, kindness, goodness, faithfulness, gentleness, and self-control.

What would be a better description of a free person than the fruit of Christ's Spirit? Free to give love, experience and share joy, abide in peace, have patience with oneself and others, to be kind in spite of people's weaknesses and failures, maintain a consistency of goodness in the changing circumstances of life, express faithfulness to Christ, oneself and other people, be gentle in judgments and attitudes toward others, and be under control because of a liberating commitment to Christ as an obedient bond servant. That's freedom indeed! Our emotions are taken captive by the infusion and guidance of the indwelling Christ.

Now we must face the question: If Christ offers us the status, security, and strength of true freedom, why are so few Christians free? Look at it this way. Our minds are like a garden filled with flowers and weeds. We need to pull out the noxious weeds that are contrary to the life, message, death, and resurrection of Christ. A mind filled with Christ's truth is a place where freedom can flourish, a setting where emotional peace can grow.

We Are Loved

The other day I visited with a friend who is usually very grim and negative. Talking with him is usually down-time. But this time he was completely different. His face was radiant, his voice had a lilt to it, and he was full of fun. "What happened to you?" I asked. He burst out the good news, "She loves me!" The man had been dating a woman for years. She had been reluctant to express her love and commit herself to marriage. When she had, it transformed the man's thinking about his life and his future. "It's amazing! Being loved, really knowing you're loved, gives me a wonderful feeling of freedom." Love had given him self-esteem, relaxed his inner tension, and lifted the grimness of his attitudes.

Now multiply the finest expression of human love ten million times and you have just begun to experience the unlimited love the Lord has for us. Thinking about that love, building our whole lives around it, makes us joyous people who are free to enjoy life. It makes us free to give ourselves away, free to care, free to dare.

Whatever keeps us from receiving and enjoying that love is sin. Sin is separation, missing the mark. We were created to live in intimate oneness with the Lord. We lose our freedom whenever anything blocks the free flow of His Spirit in us.

Jesus clarified this with a very pointed illustration of the difference between being a slave and a son. "Most assuredly, I say to you, whoever commits sin is a slave of sin. And a slave does not abide in the house forever, but a son abides forever. Therefore if the Son makes you free, you shall be free indeed" (John 8:34-36).

Remember that this was spoken to the Pharisees who had great pride in their heritage as the people of God. But rite, ritual, and regulation had taken the place of profound relationship with the Lord God. They were separated from Him by pride of their own efforts to justify themselves by their own goodness. The result was that they were living as slaves because of their compulsive patterns.

Many of us can identify with that. We become so dependent on our assumed status with God that we negate our calling to be recipients of His grace as loved and forgiven sons and daughters of our heavenly Father. Jesus clearly asserts His messianic status as the Son of God and reminds the Jews, and us, that He has come to return us to the true freedom— acceptance in God's family.

A Hebrew slave served a Hebrew master for only seven years and then was released. He was sent away from the master's house. Jesus contrasts that with abiding as a child of God forever. Then boldly He claims that only *the* Son can make us sons and daughters.

How will He do it? How does He do it for us? Through the one, never to be repeated, substituting sacrifice of the cross. We'll be talking about the implication of that in subsequent chapters of this book. What we need to stress now is that you and I have been adopted by the Lord. We are loved unreservedly, in spite of anything we've said or done. We will feel free when our minds are controlled by that liberating truth. His love will never ebb or subside. And really knowing that makes us free indeed. Jesus' word "indeed" means superlative freedom, more than we could ever earn or deserve. Knowing that truth, thinking it through, and recognizing it as the basis of all our responses to life is the beginning of the growing process of becoming truly free people.

In this passage we are considering—John 8:31-36— it is important to emphasize that Jesus used the idea of knowing truth in the Hebrew understanding of the Hebrew verb "to know." That was very different from the Greek idea of knowing. The Greeks thought of knowledge in terms of ideas, theories, and philosophical verities. The Hebrew meaning of knowledge went much deeper. To know something required the total involvement of the entire person. In fact, "to know" was used to describe the complete union of a man and a woman in marriage— oneness of mind, heart, will, and body. That's the deeper sense in which we must consider how knowing the truth involves the thinking brain and its powers of memory, imagination, and will. Such knowing calls into action the whole nervous system, our emotions, and our physical bodies. The truth of our liberation through Christ's life, death, resurrection, and indwelling power becomes the unifying factor of our total existence.

How can this happen? It happens only as we experience the inseparable relationship between Jesus' promises: "The truth shall set you free" and "If the Son makes you free, you shall be free indeed." *The truth that sets us free is Christ Himself.* We cannot discover true freedom at an independent distance from Him. Dean W.R. Inge was right, "Christianity promises to make men free; it never promises to make them independent." It is in an open, honest, intimate relationship with the Truth Himself that we are set free.

The theme of this book is freedom in the Spirit. We have talked about the meaning of freedom. Now we must turn our attention to the Spirit. The indwelling Spirit of Christ is the source of a consistent, artesian flow of the thought and feeling of freedom.

And yet many of us have a shell around the citadel of our self. That shell must be broken open before we can receive Christ, His truth, and lasting freedom. How can that take place?

2

Broken Open, Filled, and Set Free

Chapter Two

Broken Open,
Filled, and Set Free

Brokenness builds. Those words may seem contradictory to you. How can breaking be constructive? Allow me to explain. I believe personal brokenness is the secret of freedom in the Spirit.

Who Is In Control?

Whatever happens that breaks us open to a deeper invasion of the Lord's Spirit is a blessing in disguise. Whenever we face difficulties and problems that break our willfulness or arrogant control of our lives it is a gift. My father used to say that troubles will either break us or make us. Over thirty years of living as a Christian has convinced me that they do both. Troubles bring us to the frayed end of our tether and force us to let go of the tight grip we hold on life. Only then can the everlasting arms catch and hold us.

When I became a Christian, I accepted Christ as my Lord and Savior. He came to abide in me. But I was not free because I allowed so little room for Him. His efforts at personality reconstruction and mind reorientation were resisted. I called on His help when I felt I needed Him. Then one day when I faced a personal crisis, my prayers for His help seemed unheeded and unanswered. I continued to pray faithfully. Still no response. For days I was left to ache and hurt.

Then it dawned on me that greater than my need for the Lord's help was my need for the Lord Himself. Broken in my willful efforts to get Him to do what I thought He should do to help me, I cried out, "Lord, I need You! Forgive me for trying to run my own life and seeking Your power for my purposes. I surrender myself and this seemingly unsolvable problem to You."

After that prayer, I felt the surging infilling of His Spirit. The problem was subsequently solved by His intervention. But the greater problem inside of me— my willfulness—was exposed and I allowed more of the Lord's Spirit to pervade my mind and heart. The Lord, who had established a relationship with me when I became a Christian, was moving to claim more of my mind, emotions, and will that belonged to Him.

You would think that having discovered that secret, the rest of my Christian experience would have been easy and filled with freedom. Not so. The person I gave Christ when I became a Christian was very insecure. I covered that with a bravado that contradicted how unsure I was of myself and the talents

He had given me. To hide my inner emptiness, I polished the exterior. That put people off and kept them from me. I wanted to be adequate. Accepting Christ changed the goals of my life, but I attempted to accomplish them on my own strength, education, and personality prowess. This came across as self-sufficiency, lack of humility, and studied adequacy. It was all a cover-up. Then, in those early years, the Lord began a character transplant and a personality reconstruction. He did it not by telling me how bad I was, but by showing me how much He loved me.

Each failure in my relationships broke my false pride and opened me further to the Lord's Spirit. His most valued gift in those days was self-honesty. I was freed of blaming people and began to ask Him what it was in me that had caused the difficulty. He was often more ready to tell me than I was to hear. But the miracle had begun. I wanted to be filled with more and more of His Spirit. Each breaking of the old patterns of my personality allowed Him greater access to me. He wanted to reconstruct the channel through which He could pour His supernatural power. I began to experience the sheer delight of being used and giving the credit and glory to the Spirit.

I am thankful that much of the basic transformation took place before an active, full-time ministry. But the breaking to build has continued through the years as I yield more of myself to more of Christ's indwelling Spirit.

And He's not finished. The other night I was awakened by concern over four major problems I had been wrestling with for days. One related to my work, another to a concern over a member of my family, another over a friend, and still another over a broken relationship. In the long hours of tossing and turning I finally prayed.

The Lord showed me how I was trying to solve these problems on my own and revealed how I had actually contributed to a couple of them with my own attitudes. He helped me see in my mind's eye some destructive attitudes and revealed a picture of how He wanted me to act and react the next day. Again self-sufficiency was broken. Another strand of the bind of willfulness was severed. Once more, a fresh infilling of the Lord's Spirit resulted.

I slept the rest of the night and arose refreshed, aware of the power of His Spirit. That day, equipped with the fruit of His implanted character and His gifts of wisdom and faith, I became a partner in the solution of many of the concerns that had awakened me in distress.

As I went through the day I was a different person. More of me was open to the Spirit and having greater access to me, He did through me what I could not have done alone. Again I was broken open to be built up in another further step in becoming a free person.

Broken To Grow

There is a three-step process that takes place when we are broken by what we've done, or our impotence in life's problems and perplexities. First, confession of our failure or our need opens us to the Lord's presence and power. Second, we cry out for the Holy Spirit to fill our emptiness or inadequacy. Third, we discover the secret that brokenness, total willingness, provides the qualification for a fresh filling of the Holy Spirit. The difficulties through which we pass in this process become occasions of blessing. Our brokenness becomes the threshold of growth in a Spirit-filled life and greater freedom.

Jesus explained the secret of this in John 12:24,25. "Most assuredly, I say to you, unless a grain of wheat falls into the ground and dies, it remains alone; but if it dies, it produces much grain. He who loves his life will lose it, and he who hates his life in this world will keep it for eternal life." A grain of wheat has a hard shell protecting the wheat germ. The germ cannot grow until the shell is broken open. This happens when the grain is put into the earth. The moisture and warmth of the earth softens it, cracks it open, and the germ begins to grow. The result? The fruit of the strong stalk of wheat that grows and ripens until it is ready for the harvest.

This parabolic truth shows us how we are broken open and filled by the Spirit. At conversion to Christ, His Spirit enters us. But His abiding presence cannot grow until the shell of our preconceptions, values, and personality structure is broken open. That explains why so many Christians remain immature and do not realize the freedom of the Spirit.

Does the Lord ever give up? No, He persists. He will never leave us or forsake us, as He promised in Hebrews 13:5. We need not pray as King David did, "Do not cast me away from Your presence, and do not take Your Holy Spirit from me" (Psalm 51:11). David's plea from his abyss of sin and self-condemnation was a projection of human attitudes onto God. By all human evaluation, God had every right to turn away from David and depart. David's panic was probably based on what he had observed happen to his predecessor Saul. First Samuel 16:14 says, "...The Spirit of the Lord departed from Saul...." But close study of Saul reveals that Saul departed from the Spirit and persistently resisted being broken of his willfulness. He refused to realize what David found in the sacrifices of a broken spirit, a broken and contrite heart. To the very end Saul was in charge of Saul. He blamed his problems on everyone else, including David. Saul had problems with Saul which he called Samuel, Jonathan, and the shepherd warrior. His final act of imperious self-determination was to commit suicide. The Lord saved David from that fate. David's brokenness was the prelude to a deeper oneness with his Lord. And the Lord wants nothing less for you and me.

Brokenness seems like a cruel word. We use it to describe someone who is deeply dejected by life's tragedies. Or it is used to describe the domesticating of a young colt. But neither use is devoid of the positive benefit which can result. I do not know of any Christians who have grown in freedom without passing through a time of realizing the futility of putting ultimate trust in their own strength, people's reliability, or dependence on circumstances. Eventually the chains to those false gods must be broken. And further, a wild colt does not fulfill its greater purpose until it is saddled, ridden, and comes under the guidance of the bit and reins. We do not discover our destiny until the reins of the Master control our lives.

Jesus called for absolute obedience. After telling the parable of the grain of wheat falling into the ground, He made an ultimate claim on us. At first it seems severe. "He who loves his life will lose it, and he who hates his life in this world will keep it for eternal life" (John 12:25). What does that mean for our growing experience of freedom? A great deal. Jesus was not calling for self-condemnation as a virtue of discipleship. The Greek word "hate" used to

capture the Lord's meaning is *misōn* from *miseō*. W.E.
Vine states that the word is often used to express
"relative preference for one thing over another, by
way of expressing either aversion from, or disregard
for, the claims of one person or thing relatively to
those of another, as in Matthew 6:24, and Luke 16:13,
as to the impossibility of serving two 'masters'; Luke
14:26 as to the claims of parents relatively to those
of Christ; John 12:25 of disregard for one's life
relatively to the claims of Christ."[1]

Jesus was not against authentic self-esteem. He
specifically said we were to love our neighbor as
ourselves. What He meant in this penetrating statement of John 12:25 was that His ultimate claim on
our lives was for us to love Him and to be His faithful
disciples. The progressive breaking of the shell of
willful self-control takes place as we die to our own
will, plans, priorities, and goals, and accept in their
place Christ, His indwelling Spirit, and His direction
of our lives. That surrender and relinquishment is
what brokenness that builds is all about.

And the reward? More than we dare expect or
imagine. Press on to what follows Christ's call to obedience. In John 12:26 He says, "If anyone serves Me,
let him follow Me; and where I am, there My servant will be also. If anyone serves Me, him My
Father will honor." The promise is that we will know
sublime companionship with Christ. And the
"honor" we will receive is to be filled with His Spirit.

The post resurrection miracle is implied. After
Jesus Christ completed the atonement of the cross

---

[1]   W.E. Vine, *Expository Bictionary of Bible Words* (Marshall,
Morgan and Scot: London, 1981), p. 198.

and accomplished the victory of the resurrection, He ascended to heaven and was glorified. Then, as He had promised, He returned to continue what He had begun in the incarnation. He came again to be the regenerator of a new humanity. The risen, reigning Christ filled His followers with His own Spirit. That's the honor that is ours. When He dwells within us He makes us like Himself and equips us to do what He did. Each experience of being broken open further prepares us for a more complete filling of His Spirit. The secret of repeated and consistent filling is the brokenness which opens us to a greater infusion. Whatever breaks the impediment of self-sufficiency enables the freedom of the Spirit of Christ in us.

Christ's Spirit With Us

The Holy Spirit is Christ's Spirit with us and in us. There's a great need today to reaffirm the oneness of God, Christ, and the Spirit. So often the Holy Spirit is thought of as a separate power apart from Christ. In the context of our discussion of brokenness that builds, we need to understand Who fills us and what happens as a result.

God is Spirit. He is the living, acting Lord of all. In creation, He transmitted His life through His life-giving Spirit. Through His Spirit, He sustains His creation with providential care. As Spirit, God created humankind and breathed into him the breath of life. The Hebrew word for Spirit is *ruach,* meaning wind or breath. The Old Testament is the stirring account of how through His Spirit the Lord called out of humankind a people to be His chosen and cherished people. They were blessed to become a channel of blessing to all people. By the Spirit, prophets were called and empowered and kings anointed. The Holy Spirit is referred to repeatedly as the presence of the Lord with His people, the source of wisdom and strength, victory in battle, and prosperity in the gift of life.

We know well the sad account of Israel's rebellion against the Lord, His commandments, and the guidance of His Spirit. At the lowest ebb of Israel's demise, the prophets predicted the coming of the Messiah when the Lord would again pour out His Spirit.

In the fullness of time, God Himself came to dwell among us. The incarnation, atonement, and resurrection was His Spirit in Jesus Christ reconciling a broken humanity. From then on the portrait of the Father and His Spirit is focused in the Messiah, the Anointed One. Jesus Christ is the acting God in the world. After the ascension Christ continued His ministry. This is in keeping with Christ's promises before His crucifixion. He said He would come to His followers; He would abide in them and they in Him; He would grant whatever was asked in His name.

That's exactly what happened at Pentecost. Without losing oneness, He was the imminent indwelling Lord. "At that day you will know that I am in My Father, and you in Me, and I in you" (John 14:20). This explains the power of the early followers of the risen, reigning, indwelling Christ. The days Christ's followers waited in the Upper Room were days of brokenness in preparation for Christ's return. That brokenness had to occur within the disciples, between them, and in their relationship with the crucified, risen, and ascended Christ.

In their own hearts the disciples had to face their

impotence without the Lord. They had received a clear call to follow the Lord and had witnessed His power in His message, miracles, atoning death, and victorious resurrection. Each had heard the awesome challenge to go preach, teach, and heal in Jesus' name. But they knew they could not begin to implement their mission without His presence and power. The time of waiting convinced them they could not make it alone.

Waiting for the Lord's empowerment for the task He gives us to do can be excruciating. But it prepares us to be willing to do His work by His power. Each of the disciples had joined Jesus' band of disciples with an inner agenda of what he wanted and needed from the Master. Some had tried to manipulate Him to mold His ministry around their preconceptions. It didn't work. And the final steps of preparation for doing things in His way, in His timing, and by His power was taking place as they waited.

But there was also a brokenness that had to happen between the disciples. Prior to the crucifixion and resurrection the disciples vied with each other for power. James and John wanted seats of honor in Christ's kingdom (Matthew 20:21). Peter's quest for power and then his denial of the Lord must have caused tensions which needed to be reconciled. Thomas must have needed acceptance and a chance for a new beginning after His persistent doubts. I am convinced that mutual confession and restitution must have been taking place during those days of waiting for the Lord's promised return in the Spirit.

Added to that, the relationship between the disciples and Mary and Jesus' family had been strained all through the Lord's ministry. Surely that was broken open and healed. And then, what about people like Nicodemus, the Pharisee and member of the Sanhedrin, who had been a secret follower of the Lord? Or Joseph of Arimathea, who provided a tomb for His burial? Could they be trusted? Also among the 120 waiting there in the Upper Room were people who had been forgiven and healed by Jesus. They must have presented a challenge to the disciples. Before, they had related to them through Jesus. Now, they had to relate on the common level ground of all being sinners whom the Lord had loved and forgiven.

The most crucial aspect of those waiting days was the disturbing contrast between Jesus' promises of what they would be able to do and their haunting sense of inadequacy. Any vestige of self-sufficiency drained out of them. They had a challenge but no courage, a purpose but no power. That made them ready, open, willing. And that's when the Lord came and filled them with His Spirit. The infilling of His Spirit released His power for regeneration and new life. The promise of John 14:12-14 became a reality: "Most assuredly, I say to you, he who believes in Me, the works that I do he will do also; and greater works than these he will do, because I go to My Father." Then to accomplish that, a further promise: "And whatever you ask in My name, *that I will do,* that the Father may be glorified in the Son. If you ask anything in My name, *I will do it* [italics added]."

Put another way, using the concept of the Logos, the Word through whom all things were made dwelt among us as recreator of a new humanity and took up His post-resurrection dwelling in His people as sanctifier to infuse His likeness into their character. The apostles became examples of authentic freedom. Their willful determination to manipulate and control Christ was broken. They were powerless to live the new life to which they were called until Christ came to abide in them. Then, filled with His power, they became the most free people history has known.

The epistles are brimming with teachings about the same power being available to us. Quoting a few of the statements concerning Christ's Spirit helps to keep our thinking straight.

Romans 8:9 emphasizes the continuing ministry of the resurrected Christ. "But you are not in the flesh but in the Spirit, if indeed the Spirit of God dwells in you. Now if anyone does not have the Spirit of Christ, he is not His."

In 2 Corinthians 3:17,18 and 4:5,6, Paul speaks of Christ as Lord. "Now the Lord is the Spirit; and where the Spirit of the Lord is, there is liberty. But we all, with unveiled face, beholding as in a mirror the glory of the Lord, are being transformed into the same image from glory to glory, just as by the Spirit of the Lord . . . . For we do not preach ourselves, but *Christ Jesus the Lord,* and ourselves your servants for Jesus' sake. For it is the God who commanded light to shine out of darkness who has shone in our hearts to give the light of the knowledge of the glory of God in the face of Jesus Christ [italics added]."

Galatians 4:6,7 is a further reference that heightens our assurance of freedom based on the firm conviction of who we are and to whom we belong. "And because you are sons, God has sent forth the Spirit of His Son into your hearts, crying out, 'Abba, Father!' Therefore you are no longer a slave but a son, and if a son, then an heir of God through Christ."

True Freedom

True freedom is experienced when we know that

Christ in us will be sufficient for all of life's challenges and difficulties. Each new experience gives us an opportunity to be broken open further to greater realization of His fullness.

We hear a great deal today about the baptism of the Holy Spirit and being filled with the Spirit. Many believe that the baptism of the Spirit is always subsequent to conversion and the filling of the Spirit is something different than growth in union with the indwelling Christ. My conviction is that at conversion we receive Christ's Spirit. Then, subsequently, we are broken open to new infillings of His Spirit. Each ushers us into greater freedom as we receive power to think His thoughts and live dependently *and* expectantly on His power.

Paul admonished the Ephesians to ''. . . be filled with the Spirit'' (Ephesians 5:18). The verb is in the present passive imperative. It does not mean a once-for-all filling. If that were the case the aorist form of the verb would have been used indicating a completed action in the past. Rather, the apostle urges the Ephesians to ''continue to allow the Spirit to fill you.'' The passive emphasizes something which is done to us rather than something we do. Every day, in each hour, when life stretches us with problems, difficulties, and challenges beyond us, we are to allow Christ to fill us with His Spirit. And when we fail or are conscious of our inadequacy, we are given a sublime chance to be broken open to new infilling.

John Calvin in his *Institutes* says, ''First we must understand that as long as Christ remains outside of us, and we are separated from Him, all that He has suffered and done for the salvation of the human race remains useless and of no value to us.''[2] Karl Barth in *Church Dogmatics* (Volume 4) speaks of the Spirit as "no other than the presence and action of Jesus Christ Himself: His stretched-out arm; He Himself in the power of His resurrection, i.e., in the power of His revelation as it begins in and with the power of His resurrection and continues its work from this point."[3] The resurrected Christ fills us, gives us the gifts of the Spirit (1 Corinthians 12), transforms us with the fruit of the Spirit (Galatians 5:22,23), and enables us to become dynamic people—". . . Christ in you the hope of glory" (Colossians 1:27).

In my own experience, the gifts of the Spirit were imparted as the result of the brokenness of realizing that I could not make it on my own. Any evidence of the fruit of Christ's character has come when I failed on my own to produce authentic love, joy, peace, longsuffering, kindness, goodness, faithfulness, gentleness, and self-control. I discovered that Christlikeness is bestowed as my heart is open for Christ's Spirit to guide and strengthen me.

The reason I put such a strong emphasis on the oneness of the Holy Spirit and the living Christ is that when the Spirit is considered apart from Christ it leads to self-centered spiritualism. Christ is relegated to a historic figure of the past who won our salvation, and the Holy Spirit becomes a private possession often used as the basis of judging those who have or have not been blessed.

The spiritual gifts are for all believers in whom Christ lives. They are equipment for ministry and

---

[2] John Calvin, *Institutes of the Christian Religion* (The Westminster Press: Philadelphia, 1960), Book III, Chap. I, Paragraph 1, p. 537.

[3] Karl Barth, *Church Dogmatics,* English Translation, Vol. IV (T. and T. Clark: Edinburgh, Scotland, 1957), p. 322.

release for praise. According to Ephesians 4:8-12, the one who led captivity captive gave gifts to men. And those gifts are for all who are consistently filled with Christ's Spirit.

A final, personal word. Where are you feeling brokenness right now? Ask the Lord to help you identify it, give it to Him, and He will fill the pain of your hurts and will heal the frustration of your unfulfilled hopes. Instead of just receiving His help, you will be filled with Him!

Here's a prayer I find helpful in claiming freedom in the Spirit:

> Indwelling Christ, You promised to abide in me. You assured me that You will be with me and in me and that You would never leave me or forsake me. I believe in You as Lord and Savior and baptizer with Your Spirit. Use whatever happens to or around me to open me further to the effusion of Your Spirit. You don't have to break me Lord; life does that constantly. All I ask is that You use my times of brokenness to fill me more fully with Your Spirit. Fill me and set me free.

3

The Freedom To Forgive

Chapter Three

The Freedom To Forgive

I have a miniature hand computer on which I figure my finances and store personal data for ready reference. Even though it is only six inches long and an inch and a half high, it's amazing how much information can be typed into the memory factors of this mechanical brain.

The Wonderful Button

On the left side of the tiny keyboard is a magnificent and powerful button. It is called the clear button. When I make a mistake in typing an entry, a touch on the clear button eliminates it immediately. Also, any information I have stored which is incorrect or no longer useful, can be brought up out of the little computer's trusty memory and wiped out forever. It is as if it had never been entered.

Each time I use this handy computer, I am reminded of how much it's like the thinking brain. It has the capacity to store up good and bad memories. How often I wish I had a clear button to press to immediately correct my mistakes, or that I had the capacity to bring up old memories that disturb me, and have them taken away, never to be thought about again.

Then, as I contemplate how wonderful that would be, I am reminded that the Lord has built into us a clear button. It's called forgiveness. When we accept His forgiveness, we can forgive ourselves, and then out of the assurance of that grace, forgive others.

The question I want to grapple with is why we use the clear button of forgiveness so little. Why is it so difficult for us to accept the Lord's forgiveness? So hard to forgive ourselves and others?

Many of us are haunted by the memories of our sins, failures, and mistakes. Even though we know about God's forgiveness, we are hard on ourselves and the people whose actions and words have hurt us. The computer of the cerebral cortex is jammed full of memory factors of the wrongs we've done and wrongs others have done to us. We constantly press the recall button, bringing up the stored memories to be displayed on the video screen of our conscious thinking, but seldom press the clear button of forgiveness.

The result is that we are not free. The thinking brain triggers the emotions of discouraging self-incrimination over past failures. When memories of what people have done or said to us are stirred, we have all the same feelings as if the events had happened in the present moment. Why don't we love ourselves enough to press the forgiveness button and get rid of it all? What Archbishop R.C. Trench asked about prayer in general, we ask about specific prayers for forgiveness.

> Why, therefore, should we do ourselves this wrong,
> Or others, that we are not always strong.
> That we are ever overborne with care,
> That we should ever weak or heartless be,
> Anxious or troubled, when with us is prayer,
> And joy and strength and courage are with Thee!

And I'd add grace, mercy, and forgiveness. What is it about us that these blessings are so difficult for us to claim for ourselves and communicate to others?

Right and Wrong

The reason is that although we are made in the image of God, we have not been transformed by a liberating knowledge and experience of the nature of God. We have His integrity, His uprightness imprinted upon us, but have not fully accepted His forgiveness for our failures to live that integrity faithfully and obediently.

Think of it this way. God created us with the capacity of learning right and wrong. In the thinking brain there is a potential repository which can be filled with instructions of how the Lord wants us to live. This God-given conscience is developed on the basis of what we are taught by parents and value-determining teachers in our formative years. The Lord, utilizing the capacity He had given us to discern right from wrong, also gave us the Ten Commandments as the essential law He wanted us to obey in living with Him and others. These commandments became the God-implanted fiber of the conscience of the people of God. The "Thou shalts" and "Thou shalt nots" became the basis of a right relationship with Him.

Sin is breaking the law of God. The problem is: what to do when we or others fail to obey His law? Our sense of integrity leads us to judgment on ourselves and condemnation of others. Blame and punishment follow irrevocably. We have done wrong or have been wronged. Our inherited sense of justice cannot easily be set aside. The punishment of ourselves is expressed in self-negation which produces the feeling of guilt. Likewise, the punishment of others who have harmed or hurt us is expressed in rejection, anger, and withheld approval. Someone has to pay!

Our problem with the wrong we and others do is the same as God's problem with us. How can He overlook our blatant or subtle sins? Added to the actual or attitudinal breaking of the Commandments are the deeper sins of refusing His guidance, living on our own cleverness, and the pride of running our own lives. The Lord cannot contradict His righteous justice and wink at our rebellion which hurts us and breaks His heart. And yet, He knows what our guilt over our failures does to us. It makes us either aggressive in our efforts to justify ourselves or weakened by self-condemnation. His justice makes it impossible to say, "Don't worry, it doesn't matter." Think of the moral chaos we'd have if He did. And imprinted with His righteousness, we cannot easily forgive ourselves or others. Our problem is really the same as God's problem.

How can God reconcile the sinner without approving of the sin? And how can we get free of the memories of our failures without denying our developed sense of right and wrong? Or how can we relate to people who have hurt us when what they did or said was a contradiction of truth and a malicious evil deed?

We Are Forgiven

Do you realize what this questioning has done for us? It has brought us into the very heart of God. Now we feel with Him the dilemma of judgment and forgiveness.

In our thinking, all too often judgment and forgiveness are separated. In God's heart, they are two sides of the same reality: His grace. The Lord had to find a way of judging sin and justifying the sinner.

Justification is the expression of God's grace. The sin must be atoned for and the sinner set free of the deserved punishment.

That's what justification is: the complete and unconditional exoneration of the sinner. The only way for God to accomplish that was to provide a just recompense for sin and an effective reconciliation of the sinner. Humankind could not do that for itself. God did it!

God came in the Messiah, the Suffering Servant, the Lamb of God. His message was grace and forgiveness, His death an atonement for sin, and His resurrection a triumphant validation of His eternal power to reconcile. Through Calvary, sin was judged and paid for. Christ is our justification. And because of the cross and the shedding of Christ's blood, we *are* forgiven. More than that we are forgiven even before we sin. The cross did not change the heart of God toward us; it exposed His justice and mercy. And now we look back at Calvary and realize that the justifying exoneration that was revealed there pulsates in God's heart for you and me right now.

This is the liberating truth Paul tried to communicate in the synagogue at Pisidian Antioch when he concluded his preaching of the gospel with a succinct, bold promise. He had told the Jews who listened to him what God had done in and through the life, death, and resurrection of Christ, the Messiah. Then he concluded with this mind-reorienting truth: "Therefore let it be known to you, brethren, that through this Man is preached to you the forgiveness of sins; and by Him everyone who believes is justified from all things from which you could not be justified by the law of Moses" (Acts 13:38,39). This is the apostle's first statement of justification by faith revealed in Scripture.

The long years between Paul's conversion and the beginning of his active ministry had been spent prayerfully grappling with the awesome atonement of the cross and his own need to be forgiven and forgiving. He selected a dynamic word to express what had happened. He had been justified: declared not guilty, exonerated, and set free. The law had not done that for Saul of Tarsus. He had sought to fulfill the law's demands with impeccability. Where the law had failed him was in dealing with his own vigilant sense of justice and his failure. The guilt had made him a judgmental, severe Pharisee. His angry persecution of the church had been an expression of his own self-condemnation. And in spite of it all, the Lord had intervened, appeared to him, forgiven him, and set him free. Marcus Dodds put it vividly, "You can hear Paul's heart dancing and exalting at the thought of it; and, still more, in the experience of it. The Son had made him free."

Paul's message came burning and flaming out of the heart of a Christ-justified man. His word to the Jews at Antioch declared what he had experienced in his own life—through Christ is forgiveness of sins. Those who accepted that forgiveness by faith alone, were ushered into the eternal status of the justified. The things from which the law of Moses could not free them, Christ could. What are these things? What we talked about earlier: a condemning conscience for all the infractions of the law.

The Jews' inbred sense of integrity which demanded faithfulness had not been able to deal with their own or others' sin. Christ had done that for them. Just as God could not forgive without both judgment and atonement, so too they could not deal with their sins without some tangible punishment and exoneration. And in Christ, God had done both. He had taken the penalty and suffered for them. And then He declared them not guilty!

Only By Faith

No wonder Paul's preaching caused a stir in the synagogue there in Antioch. It was a radical truth he proclaimed. The impacted implication was that the Jews' relationship with God was not dependent on their own keeping of the law or self-incrimination when they failed. Only by faith in Christ, the justifier, could they claim their status as emancipated, totally exonerated sons and daughters of a gracious, forgiving God.

The reason many of them rejected the wondrous offer was that it threatened their whole orientation of self-generated righteousness and their self-determined judgment. Their condemnation of others had become the basis of their false superiority and exclusiveness. Self-righteousness is a demanding false god. Breaking of the first commandment to have no other gods before Yahweh makes efforts at keeping all the other commandments a brash contradiction. And where do we turn when we've broken the other nine because we have not kept the first?

Paul gives us the answer in his more complete development of the theme of justification by faith in Romans. In Romans 3:23-26, we meet God as both just and the justifier. How He maintained both positions is the exciting news Paul has to share. ". . . All have sinned and fall short of the glory of God, being justified freely by His grace through the redemption that is in Christ Jesus, whom God set forth to be a propitiation by His blood, through faith, to demonstrate His righteousness, because in His forbearance God had passed over the sins that were previously committed, to demonstrate at the present time His righteousness, that He might be just and the justifier of the one who has faith in Jesus."

Note the progression: righteousness, the just, the justifier, and faith. Righteousness is essentially the quality of being right. God's righteousness is the consistent expression of His nature. As the author of truth, He is truthful; as the source of love, He is unchangeably faithful. God is love and cannot deny His lovingkindness. But He must judge the denial of His love, untruth in any form, and all distortions of His plan and purpose for humankind set forth in the Commandments. He cannot abdicate being just, that is, the judge of all sin. The reason is that sin is contrary to His righteousness and results in separating us from the relationship of love, dependence, and trust for which He created us. What can God do? The just must also be the justifier. We cannot help ourselves with efforts to be good enough or self-justification through self-punishment. Without denying His nature as the just, God must become the justifier.

The words righteousness, the just, the justifier, and

justification all come from the same Greek root. Out of unqualified grace, our righteous God makes us right with Himself by both demanding atonement and providing it. He is both just and the justifier in the sacrifice of Calvary. Faith is the only qualification for accepting and enjoying the free gift of forgiveness and freedom. But even that cannot be deserved or earned. It too is a gift. The same Lord who is just and justifier is also the giver of the ability to respond. God enables us to accept our justification, and claim our righteousness in Him. The primary gift of His Spirit at work in us is faith. By faith alone, we claim that we are forgiven and reconciled with God. Our deepest problem, however, is living by faith and not our goodness. We continually try to earn what is a free gift.

Faith and Forgiveness

What does all this mean to us in our difficulty in accepting and imparting forgiveness? Everything! Even though we believe in Christ and know that He died for our sins, many of us have more of the justice of God ingrained into us than we have of His merciful grace. We know and emulate Him as the just but not the justifier. On a daily, experiential level, often we deal with ourselves and others as if Christ had not suffered to justify us. Because we have not allowed Him to love us sufficiently, we cannot forgive ourselves and others profoundly. Our righteous indignation makes us very hard on ourselves and stingy in our forgiveness of others.

One part of us sings, "In the cross of Christ I glory," and the other demands the quid pro quo of "an eye for an eye and a tooth for a tooth" in dealing with our failures as well as others'. And so our memories of what we and others have done are pressed down into the post-conscious reservoir. We play an "out of sight, out of mind" game that does not work. All we need is for some circumstance or situation to fumble with the recall button and it's all there to be felt with remorse or indignation all over again. The unknown poet was right:

> In our earthly temple there's a crowd
> One that's humble and one that's proud.
> One that's brokenhearted over sin;
> One that unrepentant sits and grins.
> One that loves his neighbor as himself;
> One that cares for naught but fame and self.
> From such perplexing care I could be free
> If I could determine which is me.

And how shall we determine? We come again to the cognitive basis of our freedom. It happens when we think freedom and then can forgive freely. That thinking demands the surrender of a half-truth for a whole truth. The half-truth summarizes the Lord's righteous judgment on what we've done or been. The whole truth is that we were judged and forgiven even before we sinned. To refuse to accept that awesome truth and forgive ourselves is the blasphemous attempt to play God over our own lives. We determine how much forgiveness we will accept. That is tantamount to saying that God's forgiveness is applicable to us only to the extent that we deem ourselves worthy of it.

Shocking? I think so. I've played that kind of false god over myself too many times.

A vital way to get hold of this truth of God's forgiveness is to ask ourselves some questions. Do you still harbor memories of past sins and failures? Does the recall of them make you feel fresh guilt or fresh grace? Do you ever think you have no right to give yourself permission to feel freed and released? Is there anything you have done or said that is too big for God to justify? Are you nursing any feelings of guilt right now for unconfessed or unrelinquished sins? Then think about this:

> Down beneath the shame or loss
> Sinks the plummet of the cross
> Never yet abyss was found
> Deeper than His love can sound.

Repeat that over and over again until you know it's true for those past sins or hidden sins which you've kept guarded from the love of the Savior. His judgment has already dealt with those festering memories. And His forgiveness, bought at so high a price, has taken them from His memory. We are not free, cannot feel free, until the conviction of forgiveness is the controlling condition of our minds. Jesus' words give us the content of our own words to ourselves. "Neither do I condemn you, go in peace and sin no more." List out any unrelinquished failures, mistakes or sins. Hear the Savior pronounce you, "Not guilty!" And then using your own name, say to yourself the assurance of pardon: "_____, neither do I condemn you!" We are called to be priests to our own souls, mediating the pardon of Calvary. A priest is the one who goes to the Lord on behalf of another and brings the Lord's love and forgiveness to another. Do that for yourself!

As We Forgive

Why is that so important? Simply because we cannot be free until we set others free by forgiving them.

And no one who is in the syndrome of self-incrimination and self-justification is able to be forgiving to others. Jesus put it flatly, "...To whom little is forgiven, the same loves little" (Luke 7:47). The more we receive Christ's loving forgiveness, the more forgiving we will be of others. The only aspect of the Lord's prayer Christ found it necessary to explain for emphasis was the petition, "And forgive us our debts, as we forgive our debtors." He said, "For if you forgive men their trespasses, your heavenly Father will also forgive you. But if you do not forgive men their trespasses, neither will your Father forgive your trespasses" (Matthew 6:14,15).

Isn't that a contradiction to the point I've been stating that we are already forgiven and that confession of sin and justification by faith is accepting what is already an established fact? Not so! Forgiving others is a vital part of experiencing our own forgiveness. What Jesus is saying is that we cannot appropriate the Lord's forgiveness until, and as, we forgive others. And those who say they forgive but cannot forget are simply saying in another way that they can't really forgive. A woman who had been deeply hurt by a friend and forgave, was asked, "Don't you remember the terrible things she did to you?" Her reply was, "No, all I remember is the day I decided to forgive and forget."

When the Lord justifies us, He relates to us as if we had never sinned. Nothing less is required of us. We have not forgiven a person if we keep alive the memory of what he or she has done by repeated rehearsal of the details. So often we tell people we forgive them and then continue to punish them by withholding our affirmation, assurance, and approval. We parcel out our warm affection on the basis of how much we think a person has changed or improved. The truth is that people are able to deal with their failures when we believe in them and treat them as if they had not sinned against us. Paul challenged the Ephesians to "...be kind to one another, tenderhearted, forgiving one another, just as God in Christ also forgave you" (Ephesians 4:32). Until we do we will not be free.

I overheard a conversation between two of my friends. One had forgiven the other. The man who had deeply hurt the other said, "How can you forgive me after what I've done to you?" The other said an astounding thing: "I cherish my freedom and treasure my experience of God's forgiveness too much not to!" What he meant was that unforgiven memories would hurt him more than the offender. He had come to love himself as loved by the Lord. He did not want to harbor resentment and anger because of what it would do to him. Further, he valued so much the Lord's forgiveness of him for his own sins and mistakes, that he did not want a refusal to give forgiveness to block the free flow of the Lord's forgiveness of him.

Forgive is an active and initiative verb. We do not wait for people to measure up or even ask for the forgiveness. Our challenge is to forgive, and then relate to the person as totally forgiven. Often that creates the desire in the other person to ask for forgiveness. But remember, God's forgiveness is not given because we ask, but given so that we can ask. Our unqualified love for a person will usually bring a request for our forgiveness. But our forgiveness is not to be measured by the other person's contrition. We can share our perception of what happened and how we felt without an "almighty" attitude. What's important is removing the barrier by expressing our forgiveness to the person.

Equally important is being receptive to people who come to us with a burden of how we may have hurt them. It doesn't help to justify ourselves with defensive explanations of why we did or said something. The point is how the other person feels about it. Often after we've asked forgiveness for what is perceived and the pain that was caused, there is a relaxed atmosphere in which the details can be talked out. Our calling is to be people who set others free. That's costly business at times. It means forgiving, asking to be forgiven, and working tirelessly to establish reconciliation. But we are not alone in the challenge. The Lord is with us. He will guide us in what we say in expressing forgiveness and how we respond in accepting forgiveness when we are at fault.

Every day I meet Christians who are not free because of unclaimed forgiveness of sin—their own and other people's against them. It shrivels their joy and makes them negative people. G.K. Chesterton admonished, "Let your faith be less a theory and more a love affair!" When it is, we grow more in love with the Savior each day. That love frees us to tell Him about our failures, with the assurance that nothing can ever separate us from Him.

Lori, a sincere young Christian, took these forgiveness principles seriously and wanted to be completely free of any impediment in the way of her experience of the Savior's love. She did an inventory of people in her life whose forgiveness she needed to ask and those to whom she needed to express forgiveness. It was a liberating experience. We all need to do that. Freedom in the Spirit is living in the flow of Christ into us, and through us to others. When we think freedom, rooted in our justification through faith in Christ's atonement, we will feel freely His forgiveness, and communicate it to others with accepting love. Charles Wesley gave us a song to sing to express the unfettered delight of our hearts:

> Jesus the name that charms our fears,
> That bids our sorrows cease;
> 'Tis music in the sinner's ear,
> 'Tis life and health and peace.
> He breaks the power of canceled sin,
> He sets the prisoner free.
> His blood can make the foulest clean;
> His blood availed for me.
> Hear Him ye deaf; His praise ye dumb.
> Your loosened tongues employ;
> Ye blind, behold your Savior come;
> And leap, ye lame, for joy!

Press the recall button. Is there anything in the deepest recesses of memory that needs to be brought before the Lord, the just and the justifier? Then by faith, press the clear button. What we've held against ourselves and others was never entered in the Lord's computer because of Calvary. So why keep it in yours?

4

The Bondage That Liberates

Chapter Four

The Bondage That Liberates

My friend Sam, an active leader in his church, was chafing under the responsibilities of living the Christian life. Laboring under a distorted idea of freedom, he longed to be released from Christ's challenge to love unselfishly, forgive unqualifiedly, and care sincerely about others. For a brief time, he looked wistfully at the lives of people whose license he mistook for freedom. He was tempted to join those who did what they wanted, with whomever they wanted, without any consideration of the results.

Freedom or Bondage

My friend was on the verge of throwing off his loyalty to Christ. But one night he had a dream. The Lord appeared in the dream. He stood at the foot of Sam's bed, and said to him, "My beloved, I sense you are finding it difficult and restrictive being My disciple. I have come to you tonight to release you. You are free to leave Me and follow your own desires. No longer do you need to pray, carry the responsibilities of working in your church, care for people, or give your time and money for the needs of others. I relieve you completely of any further responsibility."

The man was awestruck in his dream as the Master continued, "You have been a beloved disciple, but your heart is no longer with Me. You have a distorted idea of what it means to be free. You think you will be free if you turn your back on your commitment to Me and follow your own desires, plans, and involvements. A loyalty to tradition is all that keeps you among My followers. You have misunderstood My will for you to be rules and regulations which you resist. Because your commitment is not to Me, but to the forms of religion, you are fighting the wrong battle for the wrong reasons. I love you so much that I will not keep you against your will. You are released from any obligations of discipleship. You want to be free apart from Me. I give you the chance to discover that is no freedom at all. Now go!"

My friend awoke in a cold sweat. Suddenly he realized how much he loved and needed Christ. Life apart from Him would be no life at all. He cried out a prayer in the darkness of his bedroom. "Lord, don't leave! I do love You! I don't really want to stop being Your disciple. Take me back. I will be Your disciple forever!"

For hours after the dream, the man lay awake reflecting on his almost lifelike encounter with the Master. He knew enough about dreams to know that the conflict in his mind about freedom had invaded his dreams. A tug-of-war within him was more than his conscious mind could handle. His dream had introduced him to a greater loyalty than his desire to break loose of the inherited restrictions under which he had chafed. But he also suspected that Christ had been the initiator of that dream to clarify the real issue. The experience also alarmed him with how much he needed Christ. That night was the beginning of a new relationship with Christ. It became a turning point in his life.

Tug-of-War

A dream like that may be uncommon, but the spiritual condition that led to it is not. Many professed Christians live in what might be called a love-resistance, push-pull relationship with the Master. Their attitudes betray an ambivalent inner heart. Like my friend, many misunderstand true freedom. They resist the rigors of discipleship because they have no liberating companionship with the Savior to give them power to follow Him with joy. At times, we've all wondered what it might be like to cut loose of responsibility, muffle the voice of conscience, and do what we want. Sometimes we act like we don't want the Savior at all.

A church officer in a congregation in the Middle West bewailed the spiritual ambivalence in the members of his church. "I wonder where the wonder went?" he said colorfully. "The people in my church react to the Lord like they were being put upon; like He should be honored that they have decided to be His disciples. They react to the challenges of evangelism and stewardship with ho-hum blandness. Tradition and sameness do terrible things to blight the growth of enthusiasm. I've often thought it would be a good idea to burn the church membership rolls every year just to see how many would want to join again with a real commitment. And I wonder how many of us the Master would want. It might be a good thing if He drummed some of us out of the corps. It would wake others up to the fact tht we're acting like we never really wanted to be disciples in the first place."

That man's impatience may sound a bit severe, but it does have a ring of reality. I hear the same urgency expressed by pastors and church leaders across the nation. It is often most intense when leaders try to mobilize authentic New Testament Christianity in their churches and call members to adventuresome giving and living. The central problem of contemporary Christianity in America is exposed. Many people have settled for a facsimile of Christian freedom: running their own lives while at the same time saying they believe in Christ. That's no freedom at all! In fact, it produces a frustration inside us that results in stress and tension rather than peace and joy.

We are really blessed when the Master gives us a choice like my friend had in his dream. It stabs us awake to the fact that we do want, need, and desire the Master.

I remember a staff member in a church I served some years ago. He was negative, critical, hostile, and divisive. Nothing was right in the opinion of this cranky young man. One day I called him into my office for a chat. "My friend," I said, "I don't think we qualify to be your church. I don't measure up to be your boss. There may be someone, someplace, who does, and I want to give you the opportunity to go find him." He was astonished. "What do you mean? I want this job. I really want to work for you and with you!" My response was, "You haven't been acting like it." He was so shocked he asked for a second chance to begin acting and talking like a committed member of the team.

Strange, isn't it? The possibility of the loss of something or someone dear to us suddenly awakens us to what it or they mean to us. It happens when a loved one comes near to death and we are forced to think about what life would be without that person.

It happens between friends when conflict threatens our relationship and we picture what it would be to lose the companionship and encouragement we've enjoyed.

Or a parent complains about the demanding responsibilities of raising a child. Is it worth it—all the worry, care, thankless duties? Then the child has an accident and the young life hangs in the balance. And we cry out, as I heard a mother plead prayerfully in an emergency ward of a hospital, "Oh, Lord, give him back to me! I've complained and fretted about him and his teenage behavior. It's not been easy being his mother. All the midnight hours waiting for him to come home . . . being taken for granted in spite of all I do for him . . . the difficulty of not being understood . . . the distress of not knowing what's going on in his head . . . the lack of communication. Lord, bring them all back. I'll never complain again, if only You let him live!"

The point is clear: What happens to us when we are faced with the possible loss of a human relationship also occurs when we are forced to think about being released from the challenges and responsibilities of our discipleship to Christ.

Focused Loyalty

Thinking about discipleship to Christ has led

me to three conclusions about freedom.

First, true freedom begins and is sustained by a liberating bondage expressed in an unreserved commitment to an ultimate purpose.

Second, true freedom is expressed when love is the motivation for accomplishing that purpose.

Third, true freedom is exercised when all of life is lived in relationship to that ultimate purpose.

These three conditions of true freedom are illustrated in the greatness we admire in outstanding athletes, musicians, and artists. Excellence is achieved only after prolonged practice. Love for an endeavor presses them on through years of perfecting their ability or talent. All other interests and involvements must be secondary to keep their goal focused. When we admire their skill or ability, we are amazed at the ease with which they perform. But that freedom to excel is the result of an unshakable commitment.

The same is true for our freedom in Christ. When our ultimate desire is to know and serve Him as Lord of our lives, all secondary purposes fall into place. Our lives become focused around our basic purpose to serve Him. His love spurs us on to the goal of doing His will and growing in His likeness. No longer are our energies squandered in a multiplicity of entangling commitments. Motivated by love we are released from the need to do anything which would cripple us. We are free because we are committed. And our only question is: How can we bring all of life under His guidance and perfecting power?

The Apostle Paul puts all this into clear focus in his message to the Christians at Rome. Roman Christians had been confused about the difference between license and freedom. Some had fallen back into old sins. Their commitment to Christ was being confused by dabbling in behavior that contradicted their central loyalty to Christ. That was not Christian freedom. Paul had to clarify the issue. Note how he did it in Romans 6:15-18:

"What then? Shall we sin because we are not under law but under grace? Certainly not! Do you not know that to whom you present yourselves slaves to obey, you are that one's slaves whom you obey, whether of sin to death, or of obedience to righteousness? But God be thanked that though you were slaves of sin, yet you obeyed from the heart that form of doctrine to which you were delivered. And having been set free from sin, you became slaves of righteousness."

Paradoxically, slavery to one commitment is the secret of true freedom. Freedom is not squandering our creativity and energies in a multiplicity of directions. We are liberated to live powerful lives when our loyalty and devotion is surrendered to a purpose that is big enough to demand all that we have and are. When that purpose commands our allegiance, total attention, and unswerving devotion, we are set free of the beguiling attraction of all lesser goals. We are able to accept or reject any action or relationship in the light of that one grand commitment.

Freedom means having one Master, one controlling conscription to a vision. Everything and everyone who distracts from that goal must be set aside. All that we do in our daily lives must express that purpose. The value of any involvement or investment of time and talent must, in a discernable way, lead toward the accomplishment of this central reason for which we were born—and born again in our conversion. We are free only when we become a bond servant, a slave, of our ideal. We were created in such a way that it is only in this liberating bondage that we are free.

Do those words alarm you? Are you prompted to say, "Hold on, Lloyd, that sounds very rigid and restrictive!"? How can bondage set us free? Think what we might miss in focusing our loyalty so exclusively. And what master is sufficient to deserve that kind of commitment?

Slaves of God

Paul answers boldly. He calls Christians to be slaves of righteousness and slaves of God (Romans 6:18,22). The word "slave" has an incarcerating, constricting, limiting sound to our modern ears. How can being a slave set us free? The Greek word translated as slave in these verses in both the Revised Standard and the New King James versions is *douloi,* meaning bond servants or simply servants. In verse eighteen the verb form *douloō* is used in the aorist passive indicative, *edoulōthēte.* "You became slaves of righteousness." Earlier in his letter to the Roman Christians in Romans 1:1, Paul identified himself as a "servant of Christ." The noun is used in the singular, *doulos.* What he meant was that he and the believers to whom he wrote, were unreservedly bonded to one Master, the Lord. We are to obey Him and bring all of life into a right relationship with Him. In relational theology this is explained as living in the kingdom of right relationships with the Lord, ourselves, others, and the world. That means seeking to know and then to obey the Lord's will in all these relationships. We are to obey the Lord as King of our lives, not our wandering desires for self-satisfaction, nor for any other person as the source of our security. Loyalty to the Lord cannot be divided and given to anything or anyone else.

Being a bond servant of the Lord and righteousness means the same thing. Righteousness is what God is, in and of Himself. The word righteousness is a synonym for all the attributes of God, all rolled up into one word. His truth and goodness, His grace and mercy, His lovingkindness and forgiveness. The word is a cornucopia of meaning for our freedom.

Remember our discussion in the previous chapter? The righteousness of God was revealed in Jesus Christ's life, death, and resurrection for us. Through the Savior we are made right with God. That reconciliation sets us free to desire to live a righteous life. Our righteousness is bringing all of life into agreement with the Lord. It means adjusting the totality of our life to be an expression of His love, His commandments, and His will revealed to us in prayer and reading of the Scriptures. And the power to do that is given us in a personal relationship with the Savior. We become free when we commit our lives to Christ and invite Him to live in us and to motivate our obedience to His will. Our freedom grows when we dedicate all our intellectual, emotional, volitional, and physical energies to serve Him.

That quality of allegiance and loyalty is as foreign to our thinking today as the words slave or bond servant are to our ears. We live in a time when people are cautious about binding commitments.

The changing attitude to marriage and the family is an example of this. Couples live together unmarried, thinking that if it works out, perhaps they will get married. Recently a radiant couple came to see me for what I thought was premarital counseling. The woman spoke glowingly of their relationship.

"We've tried out living together for five years. Now we think it's time to make it official. But we're so leary of commitments. We've talked it over and want to ask you to leave out the 'as long as we both shall live' part of the vow."

The couple wanted a loophole. And so do others who experiment with extramarital relationships or dabble in what's called "open marriage," where intimacy is shared with others in addition to their mates. "No one person can have all the qualities you need!" one man said in defense of the practice.

We dare not be simplistic about the growing divorce rate, nor insensitive to the pain and anguish it has caused couples and their families. But, in addition to those who reluctantly take that step because there seems to be no way to stay together, there are countless numbers of couples who take divorce lightly as the easy alternative to lasting commitment.

The same lack of steadfastness in our commitments is found today in friendships, our loyalty to our jobs, and our participation in our churches.

So, let's admit it; Paul's call to be bond sevants to the Lord and righteousness does run counter to the mood of our contemporary society. That's why many Christians are not free. We find it difficult to make an unreserved commitment to the Lord and to bringing all of life into consistency with His purpose for us.

Being a bond servant of the Lord and righteousness go hand in hand. We can't have one without the other. Trying to live a righteous life without the Lord's indwelling power ends in futile efforts at self-generated perfectionism or religiosity, and trying to enjoy a relationship with the Lord without adjusting all of life to His will soon becomes sloppy subjectivism. The Lord says, "Do you really want to be free? Then give me your absolute commitment and together we'll shape your whole life into a joyous expression of righteousness."

And our response? George Mattheson worded a liberating one. "Make me a captive, Lord, and then I shall be free. Force me to render up my sword, and then I will conqueror be."

Free Captives

One of the most moving biblical accounts of this deeper level of freedom is what happened to the servant in Exodus 21:1-7. It was the rule in ancient Israel that a Hebrew servant could serve a Hebrew master for only seven years. During the sixth year of his service he was told that in the seventh year he would be released. But if he had come into bondage without a wife, and his master had given him a wife, he could not take with him his wife or any children born during the six years.

The Exodus account focuses on what should happen if a slave chooses not to be released but to stay with his master, wife, and children. "But if the sevant plainly says, 'I love my master, my wife, and my children; I will not go out free,' then his master shall bring him to the judges. He shall also bring him to the door, or to the doorpost, and his master shall pierce his ear with an awl; and he shall serve him forever."

Picture in your mind's eye the tender drama behind those regulations. Imagine a master and servant who have come to a relationship of mutual respect, friendship, and trust. Because of the master's kindness and the servant's faithful industriousness, a deep companionship forms. The servant has been treated like a brother and in response he has cared for the master's land, cattle, and possessions as if they were his own.

Both the master and the servant dread the ending of the seven years. The master thinks about it reluctantly. "Soon I must release my cherished servant. It will be difficult to tell him, to let him go." Likewise the servant contemplates the coming eventuality—what for other servants with hard masters is a day of liberation from bondage, he can only think of as a day of excruciating choices. If he chooses to be released he must leave his master, his beloved wife of a few brief years, and his cherished children. Release seems like the real bondage; remaining with his duties pulses with the righteousness of real freedom.

Eventually the day of choice comes. The master comes to his valued servant and says, "My dear friend, you have been more than a servant. We have worked this land as if it belonged to both of us. I've given you full responsibility and in return you've worked diligently for me. Your wife is like a daughter to me, and your children like my own grandchildren. It breaks my heart to think of you leaving me or them, but according to the law I must give you that opportunity."

The servant's response was filled with passion. "Master, I love you. I love my wife and children. How can I leave you all behind? My duty, my joy, is here. It is not freedom if I go, but a slavery!"

The ceremony of the piercing of the servant's ear with an awl must have been a jubilant celebration. The pain in the lobe of the ear lasted only for a moment, but the scar was a constant reminder that he had chosen to be free to serve his master, love and enjoy his wife, and raise his children.

The Ultimate Choice

Our commitment to the Lord must pass through the same turbulent sea of ultimate choice. We are free to leave our Master, but would that be freedom? We are released to throw off the responsibilities of being a bond servant of righteousness, but would that bring us freedom? No, but given the choice, we are introduced to the real person inside us and to what we really want. And we exclaim, "Master, there is no real freedom without You. Serving You and doing Your will is all I want!"

Truly free people have been confronted with that choice and have made a commitment to serve Christ forever. They are free because of a controlling passion for an ultimate purpose which is grand and demanding enough to call forth all they are. Then all competing, secondary loyalties are marshalled into place to march to the cadences of the Lord's drumbeat. And because we've put Christ first in our lives, we serve Him in our marriages, or singleness, families, jobs, churches, and communities in a much more creative way.

A further illustration of this awesome choice given us by the Master is in John 6:60-69. At the beginning of Jesus' ministry, there were thousands who followed Him. His magnetism, healing miracles, and messages of God's love attracted them. But when He began to talk about the cross, true discipleship, and obedience, many departed. John records with stark reality the people's response to the challenges of the Lord: "From that time many of His disciples went back and walked with Him no more."

As Jesus watched the thinning ranks of defecting

followers, He turned to the disciples and asked the question, "Do you also want to go away?" Did He see in their eyes the same desire to get out of their discipleship, to go back to their nets, tax table, or personal agendas? I think so. In a way Jesus' question was, "Some of you also are thinking about leaving, aren't you? I release you. I want you to be My followers because you want to be, not because of obligation or compulsion. You may go back to your old life."

Simon Peter spoke for the whole band of disciples. I've often wondered if they talked it over and elected Simon to speak for them. With tears streaming down his face, the disciple sobbed out the response, "Lord, to whom, shall we go? You have the words of eternal life. Also, we have come to believe and know that You are the Christ, the Son of the living God."

There we have it again. The choice of freedom in obedience to the Master. Shall we leave the Master? Where else can we go? True freedom is lost without Him!

And in our quiet contemplation the startling words sound in our own souls. The Master speaks to us. "Finding it difficult to be a Christian? Straining at the reins? Wondering what you'd do if you were not My disciple? You don't have to stay with Me. Only remain if you really want to." We close our eyes and picture Him, His winsome loving eyes beckoning us to choose true freedom committed unreservedly to Him, motivated by His love. Then we look from His face to His nail-pierced hand. In it is an awl. "Are you ready?" He asks. "Remember it's forever, but also remember that I'll be with you always."

How will you answer? How will I? The words of the Hebrew servant and the disciples seem mysteriously appropriate. "I cannot leave you, Lord; I love You. Where else can I go? I am free only in You!" And then some words from an ancient hymn, "Come, Thou Fount of Every Blessing," burst into song in our hearts and become our prayer of liberating commitment:

> O to grace how great a debtor
> Daily I'm constrained to be!
> Let Thy goodness, like a fetter,
> Bind my wandering heart to Thee!
>
> Prone to wander, Lord, I feel it,
> Prone to leave the God I love:
> Here's my heart, O take and seal it,
> Seal it for Thy courts above.

5

When We Don't Feel Free

==================== **Chapter Five**

When We Don't Feel Free

We've all experienced it. Times of great freedom followed by times when we feel anything but free. We seem to lose the release we've known, and for a time, tighten up and live grimly. Our thinking about our freedom through Christ's atonement and our justification by faith alone becomes clouded. Our attention is off Christ and back on ourselves. Life becomes a strain again. We get down on ourselves. Anxiety sets in and we begin worrying about everything and everyone. We wonder what happened to the freedom we enjoyed in the Spirit.

Chances are, we are nursing a bad case of self-condemnation which we are trying to heal with a quick-cure dose of self-justification. Both the sickness and the ineffective remedy are the result of distorted thinking.

Self-Condemnation

Self-condemnation has many causes. All of them rob us of feeling free. It may be a failure, mistake, or sin we thought we were rid of forever. "How could I have done that?" we ask ourselves indignantly, judging ourselves. Other times we entertain thoughts and plans we know the Lord cannot bless, and we are reluctant to confess. When we finally see our ideas for what they are, we accuse ourselves for even thinking such things.

And then there are those times when we get impatient with our progress as persons. We don't measure up to our own standards of perfection and demand greater and faster improvement. We become our own taskmasters and feel the whiplash of our own dissatisfaction. Then we make a fatal mistake: We project our judgment of ourselves to God. How can He love us knowing what we've been or failed to do? Our feeling of freedom slips away.

People around us are usually more than ready to contribute to our feelings of self-condemnation. They don't feel any better about themselves than we do and are wound up in judgmentalism, ready to spring on our mistakes or inadequacies.

Ever had someone in your life with the self-appointed calling to straighten you out? There are personality-remodelers everywhere. You may live with one, work with or for one, or have one among your friends. We think we can slough off their efforts to manage our lives with criticism, but what they say rankles in our minds long after they've spoken. What they say triggers our own self-doubt. "Maybe they're right," we say to ourselves. "I'm certainly not all that I ought to be." Then our minds travel down the dark corridors of our own perception of what areas in our lives need improvement. We end up in the bondage of discouragement and self-negation.

When the spiraling mood of self-condemnation hits below bottom we decide something has to be done. And our self-help cure is usually iatrogenic. An iatrogenic sickness is one that has been worsened by the practitioner. And that is what happens. Our efforts at self-justification make us more distressed spiritually than we were before.

We feel we must do something to reestablish a right relationship with the Lord. A desire to be adequate is added to justification by faith. It takes many forms: self-effort, rigorous self-improvement programs outlined in resolutions we promise ourselves we'll never break, being more religious, working harder and longer to prove our self-worth, or trying to cover our tracks by hiding our mistakes.

But through all our despair, the Lord has not changed nor has our eternal status as freed, justified people who are loved, forgiven, and accepted by God. We have tried to add methods of justifying ourselves that are both unnecessary and unproductive. For a time we have shifted from living by faith and have sought to win back our feeling of freedom by trying to set things right with the Lord by our own efforts.

By Faith Alone

What we've missed again is the truth that we cannot earn the Lord's love and approval. There's nothing we can do, say, or perform that will make Him love us more than He does already.

We are not alone in the syndrome of self-condemnation and self-justification. The problem has been around for a long time. It was the central issue Paul confronted in his epistle to the Galatians. What he wrote, particularly in Chapter 5, gives us a profound diagnosis and a lasting cure for these troublesome lapses in feeling free.

When the apostle first visited the Galatians, he preached Christ, the cross, and grace. He explained the gift of faith as the only basis of righteousness with the Lord. Many of the Galatians became Christians and experienced the freedom of being loved, forgiven, and accepted by God. Strong churches were established in the area made up of Gentiles whose status with the Lord was based on justification by faith alone. That was all Paul required. The disciplines of the Christian life flowed naturally from that faith. A personal relationship with Christ, the indwelling of His Spirit, and a life under His guidance gave them joy and spiritual freedom. Nothing else was needed.

Not so for a group of Hebrew Christian teachers who felt compelled to further instruct the Galatians after Paul left. They were called the Judaizers. Along with the Pharisees who had become Christians, and a group called the "circumcision party," they held that Gentiles could not become part of the church without first becoming full participants in the Hebrew religion. The same requirements for a Gentile to become a proselyte of Hebraism were transferred to be the minimum qualifications of becoming a Christian and a member of the church. For a Gentile male that meant circumcision and acceptance of the law of Moses, which implied not only the Ten Commandments but all the rules and regulations. The message of the Judaizers was "... unless you are circumcised according to the custom of Moses, you cannot be saved" (Acts 15:1).

We can imagine how this unsettled the new Galatian Christians. Many of them felt the impact of the judgment leveled on them by the Judaizers. They gave in to the idea that Christ and justification through Him by faith alone was not enough. The human tendency for self-condemnation was stirred in them. They wanted to be sure to please the Lord and so received initiation instruction in the law and the rite of circumcision. It was the way the law of Moses was taught then that led them astray. They were led to believe that obedience to the Ten Commandments and regulations had to be kept impeccably before they would be justified with the Lord. Self-effort rather than faith became the focus of their lives. They lost the joyous freedom they had in efforts of self-justification.

Christian Freedom

It was to correct this denial of the cross and the atonement that Paul wrote Galatians. Good thing. What the apostle wrote gives us one of his most comprehensive statements about Christian freedom. Galatians also gives us the key to unlock the self-constructed prison of self-condemnation. Like the Galatian Christians we are tempted to think that something we can do needs to be added to faith. They responded to the guilt-producing, false teaching of the Judaizers, thinking that efforts to fulfill the Commandments and the multiplicity of the regulations of Moses would more completely justify, that is, make them right with a righteous God. We do the same with the Ten Commandments, the regulations of some brands of religion, and the dictates of the culture in which we've been raised. All of these are essentially good. But they are meant to express, not establish, our righteousness with the Lord.

In the early church this issue boiled to the surface in what was called the Jerusalem Council (Acts 15). The controversy over the status of Gentile believers was confronted head-on. The question was: Could Gentiles become part of the household of God without first being instructed in the Commandments, the regulations of Moses, the traditions of Israel, and the initiation ritual of circumcision, the distinguishing mark of a Hebrew male?

Paul said, "Yes!"

The Christian Pharisees, the circumcision party, and the Judaizers said, "No!"

The issue for the Judaizers was that Jesus had come as the long expected Hebrew Messiah to redeem Israel. If they had their way, Christianity would remain a sect of Judaism. Admittance to the church for them required all of the essentials of the Hebrew religion *before* Gentiles could enter into full status as fellow believers.

Paul won out for justification alone at the Jerusalem summit meeting. But the decision of the council —not to require full initiation into Hebraism and circumcision—did not silence his antagonists. Particularly the Judaizers. They dogged the apostle's footsteps and followed his missionary preaching with zealous teaching based on the idea that faith in Christ was not enough.

When Paul realized how destructive that had been to the Galatian Gentile believers' freedom in Christ, he passionately penned his epistle to them. Galatians 5 provides us with some essential guidelines of what to do when self-justification robs us of our freedom.

The first is to *reclaim our "rebirth-right."* Paul admonishes, "Stand fast therefore in the liberty by which Christ has made us free, and do not be entangled again with a yoke of bondage [slavery]" (verse 1). When we begin to feel unfree, the place to go immediately is to the foot of the cross. When we push ourselves down with self-condemnation or others push us around with unsettling criticism, Christ's forgiveness and reconciliation is our only hope. Feelings of being unfree are an alarm signal that we need a fresh experience of grace.

The astonishing thing about most of us is that we wait too long. It's a common problem.

Recently, I spoke to a gathering of evangelical leaders. They are the spiritual giants of our time. Early in the morning as I did my final preparation, I was guided by the Lord to change my message. The clear instruction from the Lord was to preach on the theme of freedom in the Spirit through grace and justification by faith alone. I dealt with the problem of self-justification that we're discussing. After the meeting, the leaders shared with me that the emphasis on justification by faith alone was what they needed most to hear to set them free again to press on with their work, reaffirmed in their status as people who are loved unqualifiedly by God, saved by grace.

One of them shared a personal experience that had unsettled him. He had been falsely accused by a critical person. His integrity and behavior had been questioned severely. Though he knew the judgment was untrue, he was tempted to defend himself with elaborate, self-justifying explanations. That morning during my talk on grace and freedom, he had prayed, "Lord, I'm in need of Your grace and assurance. This criticism has triggered an old pattern of defensiveness. I have no security other than Your Love and the atonement of Calvary. Forgive me for muddling with this criticism, thinking I could handle it alone. I claim again the sure Rock on which I stand."

Later, the man said to me, "If I could make one wish for myself and my growth in grace, it would be that when I feel unfree, I would not wait so long before going back to the only source of healing. What I preach to others, I need most of all myself!"

Another participant in the meeting commented, "I think I discovered the reason I felt so much stress lately." She went on to explain, "I was raised in the work ethic. Whenever my relationship with the Lord becomes less than vital, I redouble my efforts. I take on an impossible load of traveling, speaking, and counseling. I came to this meeting feeling burned out. Again I had to rediscover that I'm not loved more by the Lord because of how much I do, but am able to do what He wants me to do because I am loved."

Rest for the Heavy Laden

New yokes of slavery are a beguiling temptation all through our Christian life. The self-justifying tendency in us takes on different expressions. Each false effort to make ourselves more right with the Lord has to be confronted and dealt with through a new reclaiming of His unearnable grace. That's why we need deep fellowship with Christian friends who can help us discern each new yoke of slavery and replace it with the yoke of Christ. In each instance Christ says, "Come to Me, all you who labor and are heavy laden, and I will give you rest. Take My yoke upon you and learn from Me, for I am gentle and lowly in heart, and you will find rest for your souls" (Matthew 11:28,29).

What I've spoken and written about those words of Christ, I have to recapture often when feelings of being unfree hit me. The idea behind that parabolic promise, I think, was a training yoke in which an older, stronger ox pulled in tandem with a younger, weaker ox. The trainee learned from the experienced beast who carried the responsibility for the weight and the direction in ploughing the furrow. Christ takes the heavy load and guides us along a straight path. But as often as I explain that to others, I am brought back to the fact that I assume new yokes of slavery that I try to carry alone. When I get exhausted or depleted, the Savior is always waiting with a liberating offer. "Take off that yoke. Here, join Me in Mine. I'll take the burden and the weight of your need." When I accept His offer, I am flooded with a renewed sense of freedom.

It's happened repeatedly all through my life. When I became a Christian in college, my prayer of commitment to Christ gave me a wonderful feeling of freedom. The burdens of guilt were lifted, the memory of past failures and hurts washed away. But it wasn't long before some rules-and-regulations-oriented Christians reminded me that all that joy had to be expressed in a specific code of behavior. Being a new Christian, I was vulnerable to both good and less creative teaching. What got through from these "friends" was that faith in Christ that didn't change my behavior was null and void. Surely there were things about my life that needed to be changed, but I somehow confused measuring up as a part of being loved by the Lord. I took on a yoke of slavery that I wore for several years, struggling to be a "good" Christian. It took a profound experience of the Lord's grace a few years later to exchange that yoke for the yoke of Christ.

About that time, I began growing intellectually in my faith. As I studied theology, I realized how important an orthodox, biblical faith was for my advancement in Christ and my preparation for communicating Him to others. The subtle shift that took place, however, was that orthodoxy became more important to me than Christ! I became a vigilant purist in the defense of minor doctrines. Intellectual impeccability became a new form of self-justification, a new yoke of slavery. The implication was that God would love me more if I acquired superior knowledge and insight. There's nothing wrong with loving the Lord with our minds. The danger comes when we think He has a special measure of grace for those who hold a particular theological persuasion.

For me, it took the rough and tumble of parish ministry to expose the false security of that yoke of intellectual arrogance. Real people with urgent needs broke open my heart and got me back to the basics in communicating God's love and hope rather than arguing theology.

But my perfectionist bent soon adopted another yoke. As a young clergyman, I wanted to please my church members. Many had different ideas about what a pastor should be and do, based on cultural conditioning in their past. Some wanted me to be an example of perfection to admire. That put a strong hook in my soul. Somehow, people's expectations and the Lord's got mixed up. Success was tabulated in being liked by everyone, even the Lord. Soon my freedom in Christ was threatened. I was not free to be myself and share what I was discovering in my own adventure in Christ.

That's when the experience of being broken open happened to me that I referred to earlier. I discovered I had no one to please but the Lord, and His pleasure was not dependent on my perfect performance. In a sharing group with fellow clergy, many of whom were facing the same yoke of slavery, I made a commitment to trust the Lord for my only security. The result was a profound liberation to preach the gospel with winsome joy. For that, Christ's yoke was easy.

The progress the Lord has made through the years is that He has taught me to identify new yokes of slavery more quickly. My tendency to equate God's acceptance with being a better husband, a paragon of parenthood, or a faithful friend, has been rethought. I now recognize each achievement as an expression of my status as a beloved child of God, not as a basis of security.

And so it has gone all through the passing years. Each period demanded fresh grace and justification by faith alone. At all times Christ has been constantly ready to exchange yokes, to give help, guidance, and rest.

Supply Lines of Grace

The second admonition inherent in Paul's stirring words to the Galatians in Chapter 5 of his epistle to them is: *Keep the supply lines of grace open.* "You have become estranged from Christ, you who attempt to be justified by law; you have fallen from grace" (verse 4). Careful exposition of the words "estranged" and "fallen" yield a deeper understanding of Paul's meaning. In Greek the word "estranged," *katērgethēte,* from *katargeō,* means "to be parted from" or in this instance could be translated "to be cut off." The word "fallen," *exepesate*, is from the verb *ekpiptō*, to fall out (*ek*—out; *piptō*—fall). What the apostle meant was that we can cut off the flow of grace, languish, and eventually fall from lack of nourishing, sustaining assurance. The image of a cut flower may be intended. A beautiful rose from my wife's garden is lovely, but its days are numbered. It is cut, separated from the root. We can do the same thing to the flowering of our freedom. We were not meant to make it on our own.

Some biblical expositors suggest that fallen, *ekpiptō*, means to fall off course. The image is of a ship that is thrown off its course and therefore will not make it to its port of destination. Either rendering is filled with illustrative imagery.

But whichever interpretation we choose, we are left with a question. Can we nullify the Lord's grace by our efforts to justify ourselves? No, His grace is unchanging. But we can close off our daily experience of it. The alarming thing is that we can become so habitual in our self-effort that it becomes a solidified pattern of our thinking and action. The danger is that we can become so dependent on our quest for self-generated acceptability that we no longer desire the Lord's acceptance. Self-justification dulls our need for grace until we think and act as if we were totally self-sufficient. In practice, we act and react as if we don't need the Lord at all! That kind of independence does cut off the flow of grace and our experience of freedom.

This happened to some of the Galatians. In adopting obedience to the Law and regulations they began to think that their religious perfectionism, not Christ, established and maintained their righteousness with

God. The joyous freedom they once knew faded and shriveled up like a flower on a grave days after the funeral.

But that's enough analysis of cut-flower Christians. What's the solution? How do you maintain the flow of grace from the root, to the stem, to the blossom of our freedom? My own experience and observation of others through the years have led me to several conclusions.

Prayer is the essential key. Daily and hourly prayer. In fact, making all of life a prayer puts everything into the perspective of praise, confession, intercession, and supplication. All of life is a gift of the Lord's grace. Praising Him for all that happens to and around us, the positive and the perplexing reminds us that He uses everything to make us open, receptive channels of His grace. When we fail, His grace abounds. We do not have to atone for ourselves —forgiveness is offered before we ask. When we are confronted by challenges, opportunities, or difficulties, we can spread them out before the Lord and He graciously gives us exactly what we need when we need it. And then, when people's needs distress us and we are broken in our own inability to meet their needs, we are given the assurance that our prayers for them will release the power of the Lord in their problems, illnesses, and discouragements. That's what Paul means by praying without ceasing. When we really dare to feel deeply our own and others' needs, only the Lord's grace is sufficient.

Communicating Love

But that's not all. Paul calls the Galatians, and us, *to an active ministry of expressing our faith through love.* He states the essence of our calling. "For in Christ

Jesus neither circumcision nor uncircumcision avails anything, but faith working through love" (verse 6). Another way of putting it would be: Whatever your brand of self-justification is, one form or another, it is secondary; what's important is the way you express the fact that you have been justified by communicating love. When love becomes our central calling, goal, and passion, we'll really need a flow of the Lord's grace. Nothing keeps us humble and open to our need for the Lord more than active involvement in costly loving. We can't do that on our own, nor can we ever justify ourselves by thinking we've done enough or been adequate.

The only way to carry on a ministry of initiative love is through Paul's next admonition *to walk in the Spirit* (verse 16). He reemphasizes the imperative in verse twenty-five. "If we live in the Spirit, let us also walk in the Spirit." Living in the Spirit is abiding. Jesus said, "Abide in Me, and I in you. As the branch cannot bear fruit of itself, unless it abides in the vine, neither can you, unless you abide in Me" (John 15:4). The root and fruit of freedom is stressed again in that powerful metaphor.

The Lord is faithful in loving us so we can love others. Abiding in Him is claiming that love through the cross; His abiding in us is the actual source of the authentic love we are to express. Walking in the Spirit means allowing Him to guide how, whom, and the way we love. Allow me to reiterate for an important emphasis: We do not love others to be justified; we love out of uncontainable gratitude for justification.

Paul's final admonition in Galatians, Chapter 5, deals with how we are to help other people with the problem of self-justification: *Don't justify yourself by comparing yourself with others.* "Let us not become conceited, provoking one another, envying one another" (verse 26). The meaning is painfully clear. So often we are tempted to judge our inadequacy on the basis of other people. If we get higher marks in discipleship, we luxuriate in false pride; if we fall short of others' performance, we wonder if the Lord loves us less. Sibling rivalry in the Lord's family (a church, fellowship of friends, or participation in some Christian work) is debilitating to our growth in grace. We take our signals from other people rather than from the Lord. And when we get into that comparison-game we transfer our uneasy state of grace to others. They pick up the spirit of competition and try to outdo us rather than doing what the Lord wants them to do. The best way to avoid this is to help people discover how unique they are, what their full potential is, and how much we love them in their successes and failures.

Comparisons in spirituality are not only odious, they are destructive of freedom. Motivating people by comparing them with others cripples their creativity. Our purpose is not to get people to try harder but to trust more deeply. Then what they try will be infused with the Lord's power. No one likes to be shamed into more effort by being told how much better someone else did. When we are caught in the syndrome of self-condemnation and self-justification, we can pollute our relationships and infect others with our spiritual sickness.

A mother confided, "The thing that pulled me out of the tailspin of self-justification with God is that I realized I was raising three kids to think of themselves and the Lord the way I did. When I saw what I had done to them, and what they were doing to themselves, I decided a change in my family had to begin with me!'' That resolve began a growing adventure in her and eventually in her family life.

True freedom is rooted in the cross, watered by grace, nourished by prayer, and expressed in love that releases others.

6

People Who Need People Aren't Lucky

====================== **Chapter Six**

People Who Need People
Aren't Lucky

I f I were to burst into song singing, "People who serve people are the happiest people in the world," you would probably say two things to me. First, knowing my inability to sing on-key, chances are that you would say, "Lloyd, stick to preaching and writing, and please confine your singing to the shower!" And secondly you would say, "If you must sing, please get the lyrics right. You got it all mixed up. It is, 'People who need people are the luckiest people in the world.'"

You'd be right on both counts. But my singing disability aside, I think I have rewritten the words of the popular song correctly.

Are people who need people the luckiest people in the world? I don't think so. Oh, I know what's intended: People who come to the realization that they need others are lucky. More than that, they are healthy, mature people. We were never meant to make it on our own. We are woven together into a fabric of mutual dependence. We need each other's efforts, expertise, and encouragement. None of us can live easily without the assistance, affirmation, and affection of others.

Then why change the words? Because there is a kind of need for people which becomes dangerous and debilitating. When we need people so much that their opinions and judgments of us throw us into a tailspin, we lose our freedom. When our self-worth is dependent on the approval and acceptance of others, we begin to play our lives to the wrong audience. We become people-pleasers instead of people-lovers.

Whenever we need people's acceptance so much that we make pleasing them the dominant concern of our lives, we become incarcerated in a prison of bartered love. We perform in order to assure the flow of approval. We need people so desperately that we seek to say and do what will keep them giving us what we need. We become the egotistic center around which life revolves. We need people to shore up our sagging self-esteem. We do what they want because we need them so desperately.

Love God First

The real problem, however, is that we use people to fill the sacred place in our hearts reserved only for God. When we deify people to the extent that we need their acceptance inordinately, we edge God out of His place in our lives. People who need people that much are not lucky at all. They are plagued with a spiritual hunger that is never satisifed.

Allow me to state it flatly. As long as we need people for our security and self-worth, we cannot love them. The focus is never off ourselves and on them. Our persistent thought is keeping them in line so that they will fulfill our needs. We need their approval so much that we measure all our words and actions to please them.

When we need people in this unhealthy, selfish way we give others great power over us and in reality we've asked for the worst that happens as a result. People have an innate sense of the power over us we've surrendered to them. Because they feel so little love from us, they are often negative and critical. Our response is usually so full of feeling that they soon discover how they can manipulate us with their disapproval. And so, we respond to, say, or do whatever is necessary to reestablish the acceptance we need so desperately. It becomes a revolving cycle. But the cycle is orbiting around us, not them.

Life is a struggle for power. The reason so many people do not feel free is that their need of people's assurance has led them to surrender their lives to a crippling idolatry. People, not God, become the lord of their lives.

The Lord created us to need and love Him and then to love people. He is the only Person we have to please. And when we know His pleasure in us is freely offered not because of anything we do, but out of sheer grace, we are free to become so secure in Him that we don't have to please anyone else. Thus liberated, we can focus on loving people out of the artesian flow of the Lord's love. Our deepest concern becomes how to communicate His grace rather than using people to fill our own emptiness.

Loving people instead of needing them is the

sublime level of freedom expressed by Paul in Chapter 9 of his first epistle to the Corinthians. He declares his profound love for his friends without needing anything from them. This leads to his remarkable declaration in verses 19 through 23 regarding his freedom from people to live for people.

Paul declares his liberation from all people and his commitment to be a servant of all people. Then he spells out the implication of what it means to be that kind of liberated servant. And finally, he states the purpose of his servanthood.

Consider this amazing statement: "For though I am free from all men, I have made myself a servant to all, that I might win the more; and to the Jews I became as a Jew, that I might win Jews; to those who are under the law, as under the law, that I might win those who are under the law; to those who are without law, as without law (not being without law toward God, but under law toward Christ), that I might win those who are without law; to the weak I became as weak, that I might win the weak. I have become all things to all men, that I might by all means save some. Now this I do for the gospel's sake, that I may be partaker of it with you."

Let's think about this statement so its truth can set *us* free. That leads us to pose and grapple with four questions prompted by Paul's startling statement of relational freedom. We can get to the core of what it means for us by asking:

- What does it mean to be free from people?
- What does it mean to be free for people?
- What is the purpose of this freedom?
- How can we measure the success of that quality of freedom?

Free From People

Paul had been through more than his share of people pressure. When he became a Christian, he became the focus of bitter hostility and angry hatred from his fellow Jews. They could not accept Paul, the persecutor of Christians, becoming a propagator of the Christian faith. His life was in constant danger. Wherever he went, he felt the hot blast of rejection and condemnation.

That would have been enough to deal with, but added to it was the criticism and undercutting of the Hebrew Christians we talked about who harassed his ministry to the Gentiles. Piled on top of that was the suspicion of the other apostles and leaders of the church. And to top it off, his closest friends often disagreed with him and questioned his guidance from the Lord. And yet he could say, "I am free from all men."

The only explanation for that freedom was Paul's assurance of Christ's love, forgiveness, and power. Only a person who can say, "For me to live is Christ" (Philippians 1:21), can also say, "I am free from all people." The sacred throne of the apostle's heart was occupied by the Savior. Therefore he did not need people's approval or acceptance. He had one purpose and passion: Christ! We stand in awe at the example he provides. Our temptation is to say, "Well, that's fine for Paul. He had a Damascus Road encounter with the Lord, heard His voice giving guidance and comfort in conflict, and knew supernatural strength through His indwelling power. That hasn't happened to us."

But can it? Our dependence on people's approval and our alarm when it turns to criticism or rejection makes us wonder. Most of us have to admit that we are under heavy people pressure. Our happiness is dependent on their affection, the threat of losing them is a constant fear, and any conflict with any of them forces us to realize how shabby our security really is. That usually redoubles our efforts to stabilize our life to be sure people perform in ways that give us the assurance we need. That robs us of even more freedom.

I had a dream some time ago in which I was stripped of every loved one, friend, position, ability, and opportunity I often take for granted. In the dream the Lord asked, "Am I not enough for you?" After what seemed to be anguishing hours, I could finally say, "Yes, Lord, You are my only security, hope, peace, and power." Then He graciously gave back what had been taken away.

But must we go through a dream like that or the real life experience of it to get free? Of course not. The Lord is for us, not against us. The first step to becoming free from people is to tell Him that we realize how unfree we are. Then we can confess that His sacred place in our hearts has been occupied by the people of our lives. That prepares us to begin a remedial program of transferring the dependence we've had on people to Christ alone.

That happens when we make Him, and not people, the primary focus of our attention. That means consistent times with Him each day, meditation on His Word, and ruthless honesty about those times when we shift back to needing people inordinately.

I don't think Paul became free in Christ immediately. Remember the long period between his conversion and his missionary work. And with each new difficulty with people or temptation to need them

Too much, he was forced into a deeper trust in the Savior. His time in Corinth is a good example. When the apostle was smarting under the rejection of the Jews there, the Lord spoke to him, "... Do not be afraid, but speak, and do not keep silent; for I am with you, and no one will attack you to hurt you; for I have many people in this city" (Acts 18:9,10). The same assurance was given him when friend and foe alike tried to dissuade him from his primary allegiance to Christ.

And yet, Paul's freedom was not an end in itself. It was the motivating power of a releasing commitment. Note how Paul follows the affirmation of his freedom from all people with the declaration of his dedication to be a servant. We've discussed how that liberated him to be a bond servant of Christ. Now the focus is on his servanthood to people: "I have made myself a servant of all." Paul was no longer the center of Paul's concern. Because of Christ, he sought to be to others what Christ had been to him. People's need for Christ was more important than using people to serve his needs.

We are not free until we serve. The outward expression of our freedom from people is that we commit our time, energy, resources, and thought to caring about them. That's the positive antidote to dependence on people.

We are not called to declare our freedom by telling people we don't need them or piously asserting that we are not going to be controlled any longer by their manipulative devices. Instead, our commitment to be a servant gives rise to an inner resolve to allow Christ to meet the needs which we previously depended on people to satisfy.

We are wise to avoid grandstanding pronouncements. We'll probably stumble in our first attempt to shift this focus from ourselves to others. Our well-worded declarations of freedom will come back to haunt us. Better to just do it. Our words of encouragement to others and our actions of gracious help to them will speak for themselves. Anyone who is free of people doesn't have to say it. In fact, if we are free, a good test is that we don't parade it. Paul's explanation of his servanthood came long after he had actually lived it.

Free For People

Now we are ready for our second question. What does it mean to be a servant of all? Paul helps us again. He entered into the world of the people he wanted to serve. With sensitivity and empathy, he cared about what was important to Jew and Gentile alike.

Because Christ was his security, he could observe the ceremonial rituals and customs of the Jews, his own people, so that he could earn the right to share Christ with them. He did not flaunt his freedom, but followed the commandments, the six hundred and thirteen Levitical regulations, and the customs of the oral tradition of the rabbis. He knew that none of these could save him. His salvation was through justification by faith in Christ alone.

Likewise, among the Gentiles, Paul did not insist on the religious regulations of the Hebrew religion. He was more concerned about people than majoring in the minors. He identified with people of all walks of life, all levels of intelligence, and all philosophical persuasions. For the Hebrews who became Christians, those Paul calls "the weak" because of their cultural dependence on the regulations, he did not insist on negating those regulations by his behavior. Being a servant meant putting no obstruction in the way of communicating Christ.

So often we do just the opposite. The customs and traditions of our brand of religion are more important to us than people who need Christ. What they receive from us is what's on our agenda rather than theirs. We often put more emphasis on the secondary things of our denominational procedures— theological subtleties or political convictions that we've baptized with an implied authority—than we do on the importance of God's love and grace. Often it seems that we need people's acceptance of *our* prejudices so much we keep bombarding them until we have some kind of agreement that satisfies us.

Free to Serve

Being a servant of people demands that we become focused on where the people are rather than where we need them to be. That requires the ministry of *listening with love.* Sometimes people have problems that must be taken seriously. That's where we must begin. Often we have to resist giving our carefully rehearsed theories or advice, and simply enter into their needs for practical help. Then when we've established how much we care, we'll have an opportunity to share Christ with them.

Listening with love requires scrapping our agenda and timetables. So often the look on our faces betrays our inner impatience. Though we do not say it, people hear our unarticulated restlessness. Written in our expression is, "I wish you'd stop talking so I can say what I want to say," or "Please get on with it; I have some conclusions I've been waiting to give you to straighten you out!" We are thinking so much about what we're going to say that we don't really hear what people are saying.

But often it's only further evidence of our need for people that keeps us from seeing them. Our need to be liked, or be an authority figure, or just the need to be needed, keeps us and not others at the center of our attention.

Often this leads us to rearrange people's shared needs and refocus them in the needs we have. Whatever other people say is worked around until it is an expression of what we are feeling about our own lives or relationships.

A counselor in our community who had profound needs in his own marriage projected those needs onto almost everyone he counseled. He felt that at the root of all problems were needs for affirmation, affection, and unsatisfied sexual hunger. He led his counselees into these areas so he could hear them talk about his own unresolved tensions. That may be an extreme case, and we all hope it is, but in less dramatic ways, to focus on our own needs is a temptation for all of us. We can engineer conversations to subjects dealing with our areas of expertise, interests, or problems. At a party in his own home, an author was overheard saying to his guests, ''That's enough talk about me. Let's change the subject. Now what did you think of my last book?''

Interesting people are those who communicate to others that they are interested in them. The servants of Christ are called to be that quality of interesting people. The result will be a new interest in the Christ they love and seek to communicate.

Caring follows listening. A servant of people asks the Lord for guidance about the particular people He has placed on his or her agenda. No one can care profoundly for everybody. Our task is to allow the Lord to give us the particular people who are to be the focus of our concentrated, deep caring. The group will change as some are helped and others take their place. Who are these people for you?

Caring means getting into other people's skin. It demands seeing things from their point of view, being available to help lift their burdens, and giving our time, energy, and money when it's needed.

Last week I was sitting in a restaurant having lunch. I overheard a woman in the next booth exclaim, "Listen, I couldn't care less!" I turned around and said, "About what?" Her embarrassed reply was, "It's none of your business!" Afterward, I reflected on those oft-repeated words, "I couldn't care less." I suspect the woman really meant, "I wish I didn't care so much." But her own needs to be free of caring and to be cared about were blocking her own calling to be a caring person.

From the foot of the cross looking into the face of the Savior our real question becomes, "How can I care more about people?"

Listening and caring is in preparation for the opportunity to serve people by sharing Christ's love. Introducing people to Christ is the true purpose of our servanthood.

We live in a day when great emphasis is being placed on practical ministry to people's material and social needs. The proverbial pendulum has swung away from concentrated concern for people's eternal life to attention to their temporal life. The swing was inevitable. For too long we overlooked people's suffering and disadvantaged conditions. Our real task is to minister to both spiritual and temporal needs but never trade one off for the other.

For the Gospel's Sake

That brings us to our final question. How can we measure the success of our servanthood? Paul was very clear about that. "I have become all things to all men, that I might by all means save some. Now this I do for the gospel's sake, that I may be partaker of it with you."

Everything Paul did as a servant was to "save" people. He really believed that without Christ people were lost for eternity. That prompted him to care profoundly about introducing people to Christ. But note his continuing concern for those who responded. He wanted to be a "partaker" of the gospel with them.

The Greek word he uses is *sunkoinōnos,* a compound word made up of *sun*—together with—and *koinōnos*—partner or sharer. The apostle Paul wanted to help people begin with Christ so that he could share the adventure of growing with them. He did not love people and leave them to founder. He not only helped people get on their feet spiritually, but stood with them, and then walked and ran with them in the adventure of the new life.

All this comes down to some personal questions about the depth and length of our servanthood. To whom are we listening and caring about in order to introduce them to Christ? And when they are ready, when the time is right on their timetable and not ours, are we able to present Christ, help them surrender their lives to Him, and begin an eternal relationship with Him? Have we persisted with willing help as they learned how to pray, discovered a daily time in the Scriptures, and became free people rooted in clear thinking and liberated feelings? Were we still around to help when they dealt with the things that threatened their freedom? Were we there to cheer them on when they became a servant to others the way we had been to them? The real test of our servanthood is whether our listening and caring and sharing has enabled people to lead others to Christ. Servanthood is setting people free to set others free!

Jesus washed the disciples' feet in the Upper Room and told them they were to be servants. John gives us the secret of Jesus' freedom to be a servant and the motivation of our servanthood when he says, "Jesus, knowing that the Father had given all things into His hands, and that He had come from God and was going to God, rose from supper and laid aside His garments, took a towel and girded Himself. After that, He poured water into a basin and began to wash the disciples' feet..." (John 13:3-5). Note the three salient things that prompted Jesus: Authority and power had been given to Him by the Father; He had come from God; and He was going to God.

The same is true for us through Christ. We are servants by His call. His authority is given to us. We know who we are and for what we are intended because we know from Whom our new life has come, and to Whom we will go after the brief comma of death in the paragraph of life. We are free to give ourselves away during the brief years of this on-earth portion of our eternal life.

The deepest need beneath all our needs is not for people, but to serve people. During the past five years, I've asked my congregation and my television viewers to write me their deepest needs so I could respond with messages from the Bible. In these years, I have received thousands of expressed needs. No one, however, has ever written saying, "My deepest need is to become a servant of people." And yet, so many of the other needs they describe would be solved by answering Christ's call to be a servant to those whom He places in their lives.

The awesome truth is that we were created to be servants of Christ by serving people. There's no chance of true freedom for us until that's our primary calling. Martin Luther said, "A Christian man is the most free lord of all, and subject to none; a Christian man is the most dutiful servant of all, and subject to everyone." That's the powerful paradox of the Christian life. We are freed from people to live for people. And in serving them, as if serving Christ Himself, is lasting freedom.

People who serve people are indeed the most joyful people in the world.

7

*Laugh At Yourself
& Live Care-Freely*

Chapter Seven

Laugh At Yourself And Live Care-Freely

A sure sign of our freedom is that we can laugh at ourselves. That's not been easy for me, but I'm growing in the ability to laugh at myself when I become uptight and worried over what doesn't ultimately count. That frees me to concentrate less on my mistakes and more on Christ.

Last summer I had an experience that helped me appreciate the progress the Lord is making in setting me free. I was in Scotland on a study leave and was invited to attend a very auspicious social function. The required dress for the evening was complete Highland garb, including kilts and all the accoutrements.

I had brought my kilt with me from home, but when I tried it on I realized what had fit perfectly when I was a young man did not fit around my stomach. I took the kilt to a tailor and asked him if he could fix it. He did that by letting out the pleats and taking a bit of material from each one of them to widen the entire kilt. But thinking I was going to pack the kilt to carry home in my suitcase to the United States, he sewed up all the pleats, so that they were tightly folded together in the back.

On the day of the party, I rushed to the tailor to pick up the kilt. I didn't notice that the pleats were all sewn tightly with white thread. That evening, I put it on without checking the back pleats of the kilt, finished dressing in all the proper attire, and went off to the party feeling very satisfied with the way I looked—from the front, at least. At the gathering, I stood talking to all the immaculately attired Scotsmen.

One of them walked up to me and confided, "Dr. Ogilvie, don't try to sit down in that kilt! You're all sewn in on yourself." Then he explained to my alarm that the pleats of my kilt were all tightly sewn together in very obvious white thread. Of course, I was embarrassed, and made a speedy exit to the men's room, took off the kilt, and meticulously removed all the thread. As I went through that long and laborious process, the words of my Scots friend kept going through my mind: "You're all sewn in on yourself!" Indeed I was, in more ways than the threads in the pleats of my kilt.

Then I started to laugh. Not too many years ago, something like that would have really disturbed me. Now it was a source of a good laugh at myself. I'd tried to look so proper.

When I returned to the party, I freely shared what had happened. The people at the party laughed with me. They found it great fun to laugh with a second-generation Scot who came to a party all sewn up. Think of all the delights we miss when we are uptight because of a lack of freedom, not only in life's little mishaps, but within the excruciating pressure to measure up to life's demands.

Living Care-Freely

Jesus had a rich sense of humor. Nowhere in the New Testament is it more vividly exposed than when He tried to help His followers laugh at some of their freedom-sapping cares. In the Sermon on the Mount, in the section on worry and care (Matthew 6:25-34), He enables us to poke fun at our own furtive concerns over material things, the length of our lives, and what the future holds. Careful exposition of the passage makes us laugh at ourselves. Then as the laughter releases us from taking ourselves so seriously, the deeper point the Master is making penetrates our thinking and enables greater freedom. Freedom in the Spirit means living "care-freely."

It's helpful to note the Greek word used for care in this section of the Sermon on the Mount. It is also translated as worry or anxiety in other versions. The noun is *merimna* and the verb *merimnaō,* from *merizō,* to draw in different directions, distract, or pull apart. Building on that, inordinate care is a distraction from trusting the Lord; care pulls us apart from confident trust in His provision, power, and plan. Worrisome care comes from thinking we have to handle life on our own, with our inadequate human resources. That kind of anxiety is living horizontally, flat out, depending on our own potential. That is rather laughable, isn't it?

Care About Things

First of all, Jesus says that it's ludicrous to be filled with care about material things. "Therefore I say to you, do not worry about your life, what you will eat or what you will drink; nor about your body, what you will put on. Is not life more than food and the body more than clothing? Look at the birds of the air, for they neither sow nor reap nor gather into barns; yet your heavenly Father feeds them. Are you not of more value than they?" (Matthew 6:25,26).

We smile, and then laugh, at the picture of birds sowing a wheatfield, driving the plow behind oxen, and caring for the chores of harvesting, threshing, and storing grain. Humorous indeed. Then the message: Birds are provided for by the heavenly Father. Their needs, in their realm, are met not in barns full of grain, but in seeds, roots, a drop of water on a leaf, and a worm in the ground.

Our problem in America is that what we eat, drink, and wear takes most of our average income. Our desires have expanded beyond necessities. Often an inordinate concern about what we consume and put on indicates that we are trying to fill that place in our hearts that should be reserved for the Lord alone.

How often we overeat when we are anxious, frustrated, or angry. And we can all remember when a new dress or suit made us feel more secure. Our attention to our appearance is not wrong unless over-concern becomes a substitute for the security and self-esteem the Lord promises to provide. Not even a retailored tartan kilt on a second-generation Scot who often makes too much of his heritage can do that!

But don't miss the humor in Jesus' statement, not

just about the birds, but in the absurdity of worrying about our food, drink, and apparel so much that we fail to trust the Lord with whom we will spend eternity. Humor is always just on the edge of pathos. And the pathos of missing our real reason for being born is so sad it's laughable. Perhaps that's the only way we can consider the enormity of that truth.

A good way to deal with our mixed-up priorities is to have a good laugh at how ridiculous we appear. The laughter can change our attitude and lead to a crucial commitment. To start, we probably need to bring our wants closer to our needs and then we can pray about them more honestly. And a good motive for that is to be able to have more to share with others in real need and with kingdom causes committed to introducing people to the Savior.

Care About Length of Life

But, like a really sensitive humorist, Jesus gives us just enough time for one truth to register and He's on to the next laughable question. "Which of you by worrying can add one cubit to his stature?" (verse 27). Can you imagine how the Master delivered that? I think He asked the question with a gymnastic stretch of his height that must have made people laugh. We laugh too, imagining Him posturing a cubit—eighteen inches—to His height. Perhaps someone in the front of the crowd burst out laughingly, "No one can stretch his height! A grown person is as tall as he or she will ever be." Maybe someone else leaped up on a large stone and shouted, "Look, Master, I've just grown a cubit!" If that happened, Jesus surely laughed. And so would we.

Again, while the people were laughing, Jesus went on with a laser-cut of truth. This time His metaphors pictured the short-lived flowers of the field. "...Consider the lilies of the field, how they grow: they neither toil nor spin; and yet I say to you that even Solomon in all his glory was not arrayed like one of these. Now if God so clothes the grass of the field, which today is, and tomorrow is thrown into the oven, will He not much more clothe you, O you of little faith?" (verses 28-30).

The thrust of what Jesus was saying is that we can't change the basic structure of our physical bodies by fretful care; God has wonderfully made us. We are astounded by the beauty of a flower that lives for a few days, and yet God had made us to live forever spiritually. The Master's deeper message was about more than adding to our physical stature. He wanted to expose the deeper worry over how long we live physically. That is captured in both The New International and the New American Standard versions in the translation of verse 27. "Who of you by worrying can add a single hour to his life?" (NIV).

That brings into focus how humorous and out of balance it is that we expend so much worry and anxiety about how long we will live physically and so little thought about how and where we will spend eternity. I am committed to support the scientific research and tireless care of the medical profession seeking to prolong physical life. But my primary concern is to claim my own and others' eternal security through saving faith in Christ.

I've often wondered if Jesus mimicked for emphasis the tone of care-ridden voices when He quoted the frantic, worried people. "Therefore do not worry, saying, 'What shall we eat?' or, 'What shall we drink?' or, 'What shall we wear?' " (verse 31). A wringing of His hands and a grim expression probably accompanied a shrill tone of panic as the Master dramatized for the people how they often sounded. I hope they laughed at themselves. Even picturing it, I'm laughing at myself, remembering times when my lack of trust in the Lord articulated an equally fretful question.

It must have cut into the people's pride to have Jesus remind them that as God-centered Hebrews they had become preoccupied with the same concern as the Gentiles. "For after all these things the Gentiles seek. For your heavenly Father knows that you need all these things" (verse 32). Sometimes people who make no profession of faith worry less than Christians. The only way to break cankerous care is to put the Lord at the center of our minds and the prioritizing of our desires. Jesus' secret of curing worry and care is to focus on an ultimate concern: "But seek first the kingdom of God and His righteousness, and all these things shall be added to you" (verse 33).

We are not free until we can rely on the Lord for our needs in each situation, circumstance, and relationship. We must allow Him to put into us the wisdom, love, and strength we will be called on to put out in communicating with people and in facing life's challenges. Only then can we relax and enjoy life. And added to that is the assurance that anything He withholds is for our growth and an expression of His timing.

Care About Tomorrow

To crease that thought into our brains the Master has one further laugh line. "Therefore do not worry about tomorrow, for tomorrow will worry about its own things. Sufficient for the day is its own trouble" (verse 34). We usually read that so seriously and ponderously. Actually it's very humorous. What could be more laughable than worrying so much about what might happen tomorrow that we are tied up in knots, unable to enjoy today. The humorous impact of Jesus' words is, "So I see you've run out of worries for today and have picked up a load of them about what might happen tomorrow. There's enough for each day. Do you think God is going to stop breathing tomorrow?"

Annie Johnson Flint found that God's grace was sufficient to meet troubles great and small. No one is free of difficulties and dilemma. But thank God for His grace...

Great Grace

His grace is great enough to meet the
  great things,
  The crashing waves that overwhelm the soul,
The roaring winds that leave us stunned and
  breathless,
  The sudden storms beyond our life's control.
His grace is great enough to meet the small
  things,
  The little pin-prick troubles that annoy,
The insect worries, buzzing and persistent,
  The squeaking wheels that grate upon
  our joy.

A mother of a young missionary who was going overseas into a dangerous assignment spent the last day before he left sobbing. "Mother," the young man said, "this is actually laughable! You're spending my last day here crying over the thing you always hoped I would do. Why not just enjoy today with me and do your crying tomorrow when I actually leave?"

How often we deny ourselves today's joys and opportunities because we are anxiously anticipating what might happen to us tomorrow.

Once we begin to see the humor in our attitudes in those three areas Jesus has exposed, we can begin to laugh at ourselves in much more of our daily life. People who can laugh at themselves are fun to be with. Their freedom is contagious. A person who is free to laugh at herself or himself gets a lot less criticism. Why point out faults of a person who is usually more aware of his or her goofs and laughingly tells us about them? We really break the bind of uptight perfectionism when we can laugh at the absurd things we do and say.

An Episcopal priest was ready to begin a prayer service in a large sanctuary with the customary words, "The Lord be with you," to which the people were expected to respond, "And with your spirit!" As the priest spoke into the microphone, realizing it wasn't working, he tapped and jiggled it. Thinking it was not operating, he shouted, "There's something wrong with this microphone!" As he exclaimed those words the microphone clicked on. And out of habit, the people responded, "And with your spirit!" The priest laughed uproariously and the congregation joined in, enjoying the clergyman's ability to laugh at himself. Then he said, "Indeed, there is something wrong with my spirit and with yours. And that's why we've come to pray. We all need the Lord's power and guidance. Priest and people. It's great to know that the Lord is probably laughing with us about what just happened. I'd like to join with you in praying to that kind of God. Let us pray. . . ."

Laughter loosens us up, is a healing agent, and frees us to take ourselves less seriously. So start laughing at yourself and begin living care-freely.

8

The Virus Of Philarguria

Chapter Eight

The Virus of Philarguria

A friend of mine called the other day to see how I was doing. "How's your health?" he asked. "Hope you haven't caught the new virus that's going around."

We hear a lot about new viruses these days. Medical science works diligently to keep up with diagnosing and treating them.

A Spiritual Disease

This chapter is about a spiritual virus that attacks the thinking brain. It's been around for thousands of years, but is manifested in each new generation. If you've ever had a bad case of it, or have been troubled by a prolonged battle with it, you know that it robs you of your freedom, causes fitful worry, clouds your vision, and distorts your values. It is a cause of inordinate stress, the agitation of the nervous system, and often, physical illness.

This spiritual virus in our thinking can paralyze our creativity and debilitate our peace of mind. It is a major cause of the breakdown of marriages, friendships, and business partnerships. The malady makes us irrational, emotional, and inconsistent. Most of all, it keeps many of us from enjoying abundant life in Christ and the disease is fatal to our eternal life if it captures the nerve center of our spirituality, with money becoming our lord instead of the Lord Christ.

What is this dread disease of the spirit and mind? Philarguria. Don't reach for your English dictionary for a definition. It isn't there. But if you check a biblical Greek dictionary you'll find it's a compound word made up of two good Greek words. The combination of them, however, equals trouble. *Philia* means love and *arguria,* from *arguros,* means silver, or money. Philarguria is the love of money. We've all had bouts with that virus. It is a mind and soul sickness that infects rich and poor alike.

But, before you flip past this chapter thinking it has little to do with your quest for freedom in the Spirit, hold on! You may have a low-grade case of the draining disease of philarguria without recognizing it. Some of you may be thinking, "Love money? I've never had enough of it to develop even an infatuation!" Others of you who have usually had a sufficient supply may not have realized how distressful it is to you.

Diagnosis of this spiritual virus often eludes detection. There are some probing questions that will help all of us consider the extent our freedom in Christ may be jeopardized by philarguria.

• Do you ever worry over money . . . having enough and keeping what you have?

- Is bill paying time a stressful time for you?
- What about income tax time? Ever disturbed by reading your autobiography in the cancelled checks of a year?
- Has money ever been a source of argument or misunderstanding between you and another person?
- Do you sometimes experience twinges of competition or even envy over what others earn, have inherited, or have been able to do because of money they have and you don't?
- Have you ever equated your value as a person with what you earn?
- Can you remember a time when you bought clothing or things to solve hurt feelings, setbacks, or disappointments?
- Do you ever get anxious about what inflation has done to depreciate your savings and preparation for retirement?

And here's a clincher:

- Do you spend more time thinking about money in any one day than you do in prayer?

If you said yes to one or more of these questions, you may be having more of an affair with money than you thought. And what's more, it may be a greater threat to your freedom than you realized.

Look again at the word philarguria. Note carefully the Greek word for love that is used in this compound word for love of money. It is *philia,* not *agapē. Philia* conveys the idea of give and take, bartered affection and esteem, where what is given is usually in proportion to what is expected to be received. *Agapē,* on the other hand, is unselfish love, given with no thought of a return. It is unreserved, unqualified, and uncalculating. *Philia* can be used for things, but *agapē* usually is used for persons. *Philia* is a cheap facsimile of *agapē.* And there's the rub— *philia* can block out *agapē.* In the case of money, *philia* for it can be a substitute for *agapē* to God and people. The love of money is a squandering of our ability to worship, adore, and serve God and others.

Fighting Philarguria

That's the concern of the author of Hebrews. In verses five and six of Chapter 13, he cautions against philarguria and offers a cure for it. "Let your conduct be without covetousness, and be content with such things as you have. For He Himself (the Lord) has said, 'I will never leave you nor forsake you.' So we may boldly say: 'The Lord is my helper; I will not fear. What can man do to me?' [parentheses added]."

Consideration of some of the Greek words in these verses is extremely helpful. Think with me about them, and you will see what I mean. The Greek word for conduct is *tropos,* meaning way or manner of life. The dominant note is how we live out our faith. It should be "without covetousness." That rendering of the Greek misses the strong intent. The word for without covetousness is *aphilarguros,* which means without love for money, the things it can buy, the status it provides, and the false sense of power it offers.

How can we do that? By being content with what we have. Here the word for content is *arkoumenoi,* from the verb *arkeō,* a word which also means sufficient. Our way of life should be secure in the sufficiency of the Lord's provision. That's the promise of the next sentence. "For He Himself has said, 'I will never leave you nor forsake you.' " The full impact of this statement is revealed in the Greek words for leave and forsake used to translate this Old Testament promise (Genesis 28:15, Deuteronomy 31:8, Joshua 1:5, 1 Chronicles 28:20). The word for leave is *anō* from *aniēmi,* meaning relax; and the word for forsake is *enkatalipō,* from *enkaleipō,* to leave behind. The Lord will never relax His vigilant care for us and will not forget us, leaving us behind in His plans or sufficient provision. And our response? To reaffirm the Lord as our helper. The word is *boethos,* one who runs to our cry.

In the light of that word study we can read this magnificent challenge and comfort from Hebrews as follows: "Live in a way that is free of the love of money. Be satisfied with the Lord's sufficiency. For He won't relax His care or turn away from you. Therefore, we can boldly say, 'The Lord runs to my cry. I will not be afraid. What can life do to me?' "

The implications of those words for our freedom are immense. They force us to think about how we can love the Lord with our money rather than loving money. That's the issue. When money competes with the Lord, the same static and agitation is set off in us as when we deify people and need them inordinately.

Money is congealed personality. It is personal power. The danger is that we can drift into the belief that the money belongs to us and can be spent, saved, or invested as our expression of independence. But just as there is a sacred throne in our hearts which no person should occupy in displacement of the Lord, money should never be on the throne as a source of security and self-worth that only the Lord can provide.

When it comes to money it's so easy to slip over

the invisible line between gratitude and aggrandizement. The liberating conviction that all we have belongs to the Lord can subtly be substituted with the idea that what we have has been earned by our efforts and it belongs to us. That fatal assumption sets off a chain reaction in our thinking and behavior and eventually in the loss of feeling free. We get uptight about money. Worry over getting and keeping it sets in. False security grows when we have enough, and panic engulfs us when we are short or in financial trouble. Money is in the driver's seat of our souls. Philarguria in many forms becomes our way of life. And as it grows, our freedom in the Spirit diminishes.

The tragedy is that it happens to many of us who are Christians. We believe in Christ, and yet concerns over money keep us bound up in either worry over the lack of money or a disproportionate dependence on the facsimilized security it provides. Of all the areas in our lives where we need to think clearly in order to feel free, money is one of the most crucial and most difficult.

So often the only time we talk about money in our churches is when church leaders are trying to raise money for the budget, some project, or a building program. Other times people are made to feel guilty about money rather than receiving practical help in how to glorify the Lord in their use of it. The needs of the poor are discussed in comparison to our affluence. But there is no clear teaching concerning what we could do about the needs of the world if we understood our sacred trust of money.

Freedom From the Virus

I want to suggest five steps to financial freedom. They have worked for me. The truly free people I know have taken these steps. Each step must be thought through clearly for our thinking brain to be healed of philarguria. The result is that our wills become obedient in implementing the truth and our emotions express the liberated delight of being part of the Lord's strategy in the use of money.

Step 1. Grapple with the question: Who owns us and what we earn and have? To whom does our money belong? Giving the biblical answer is easier than really living the truth it asserts.

The Bible tells us clearly that all that we have and are belongs to the Lord. We could not breathe a breath, think a thought, take advantage of our training and education, work for a wage, or receive compensation for our labors without the Lord's moment by moment provision. Deuteronomy 8:18 sounds the clarion call to think, believe, and live this truth that sets us free: "And you shall remember the Lord your God, for it is He who gives you power to get wealth, that He may establish His covenant which He swore to your fathers, as it is this day." The challenge is to remember, bring back this truth to the center of our thinking, and allow that thinking to dominate our activities. The liberating truth is that it is God who gives us power to get money.

Now, couple that conviction with the idea that what He gives us power to get is not ours but His. Psalm 24:1 is worthy of creasing into the many folds of our thinking brain. It is the sure antibiotic for the virus of philarguria: "The earth is the Lord's, and all its fullness, the world and those who dwell therein." That thought has a way of exposing all lesser ideas that what we earn and have is ours. Even the idea that what we have is ours to be used for the Lord's work must be exposed as a dangerous half-truth. All belongs to the Lord. We will not be free of financial worry or acquisitiveness until we accept that, remember it hourly, daily, and as the basic belief of our minds about money, its buying power, and its potential deification. Money must be thought of as God's or it becomes our god.

Step 2. Recognize that sincere gratitude is essential for financial freedom. Praise and thanksgiving for all that we are and have acquired keeps our thinking consistently straight. Then love becomes the liberating guide for how we use our money and what it can buy. That breaks the money bind. Payday becomes a day of thanksgiving. Out of gratitude, we become faithful stewards of all the Lord has enabled us to earn.

The Lord's grace, multiplied by our deep gratitude, equals a growth in greatness. The truly great people I know never forget to say thanks. Gratitude is the antidote to pride. The more thankful we are, the more we can enjoy what the Lord provides. We don't have to pretend a false humility. When we are delighted by what we have or when others compliment us on our accomplishments, we can point away from ourselves to the Lord who has blessed us.

Ever wonder why the Lord wants our gratitude? The Scriptures are filled with the admonitions to give thanks. Does the Lord need our gratitude? No, but He knows how much we need to express it. It is the language of a profound relationship, the expression of dependence. Thanksgiving keeps us from taking the Lord and His goodness for granted.

I have often pondered Jesus' alarm when only one of the ten lepers He had healed returned to give thanks (Luke 17:14-19). "Were there not ten cleansed? But where are the nine?" The incarnate heart of God in Jesus was alarmed. He knew that it was spiritually perilous for the nine to enjoy their new freedom from the dreaded disease of leprosy without expressing gratitude. We wonder why they were so insensitive. Perhaps they had harbored resentment about ever being sick and accepted their healing as a long overdue recompense from God. Or maybe they became so excited by the gift of healing that they simply forgot to thank the Healer. Or more likely, they became so busy making up for the lost time during their illness that they felt they had no time to go back and thank the Lord.

Could it be that the reason Jesus was so concerned about the nine lepers' lack of gratitude was because He knew that an unacknowledged blessing becomes a bane? Anytime we refuse to praise the Lord for His goodness, the blessing we've received becomes a block to further communication with Him.

The same thing is true in human relationships. When we go out of our way to help a person or provide a needed gift and there is no response of gratitude, our relationship with that person is strained. Not only are we hurt by the lack of response, but the recipient becomes uneasy in our presence. A superficial relationship results. We feel we are taken for granted.

The other day, at a community gathering, I sat next to an admiral in the Coast Guard. He is stationed in Los Angeles and is responsible for the West Coast operations of the Guard. I asked him how things were going. That brought forth the story of an experience he had that morning that distressed him. He had gone up the coast to decorate a sailor for an act of valor. The seaman had risked his life in a storm to save a man whose boat had capsized. He had pulled the man out of the sea, given him mouth-to-mouth resuscitation, and under perilous conditions had gotten him back to port and on to a hospital. When the young Coast Guardsman went to visit the survivor later in the day, he was astounded by his attitude. The man could not say thanks. Even though he was alive because of the sailor's courage in danger, he treated him with an alarming lack of appreciation. The sailor said, "Sir, I'm the man who pulled you out of the sea!" The man's only response was to talk about how bad the storm was. No thanks, no praise for the heroism. Was he embarrassed? Or did he feel the sailor had simply done his duty and needed no thanks?

The admiral went on to say that when he decorated the sailor with a medal of honor, he gave him an opportunity to respond. "Thank you, Admiral, for the honor," he said, and then blurted out, "but the man never said thanks!" The admiral shared the sailor's amazement and was still ruminating about it when we visited later that day.

I am reminded of how much we have received from the Lord and how often we neglect or resist giving thanks. That cripples our ability to receive more of what the Lord wants to give. He delights to bless a thankful person.

When we consider His gifts of life, salvation through the cross, the abundant life now and eternal life forever, the constant flow of timely interventions we have experienced in times of need, the relationships we have with loved ones and friends, we say, "Love so amazing, so divine, demands my life, my soul, my all."

Our initial commitment to Christ is refreshed repeatedly as—with thanks to God—we commit ourselves to love others as we've been loved and share the blessings we have received. Stewardship of our money is simply a way of accepting and passing on love with gratitude. That's the reason the Lord wants our thanksgiving. It produces a grand generosity in our relationships with Him and others. We become free to be transmitters of His grace.

Paul saw gratitude as an essential ingredient of the plan of God for us. "In everything give thanks; for this is the will of God in Christ Jesus for you. Do not quench the Spirit" (1 Thessalonians 5:18,19). Thanking God in all of life nourishes our relationship with Him and keeps us open to the flow of His Spirit through us. When we constantly give praise, we are capable of receiving the Lord's guidance on how to express love to others as the expression of our gratitude to Him.

Step 3. Experience financial freedom by tithing and thriving. In the Bible, tithing is not an option. From Abraham, Isaac, and Jacob, on to Moses, and then throughout the Old Testament, the Lord clearly defined the tithe as His method of computing stewardship. One hundred percent is His and we acknowledge that by returning the first tenth to Him for His work. The first tenth of all that we earn or receive from our labors belongs to the Lord. Tithing is an expression of gratitude and obedience. One who obeys is free; one who is free, obeys.

As Christians we can fulfill the Ten Commandments and the irrevocable mandates of God with freedom and joy. We are not given the option of which we will choose to follow. Biblical teaching states that the first-fruits of the harvest of our labors is not ours. It is to be returned to the Lord as our witness that we belong to Him and all that we have is a sacred trust.

Tithing breaks the philarguria membrane around our souls. It liberates us from the snares of materialism in the human kingdom of thingdom. We declare to God, ourselves, and others that we are committed, biblical stewards of all that God has provided by setting aside the tithe. Liberated Christians throughout history often have kept two sets of books: one for the tenth, and the other for the nine-tenths. God wants to guide our love-oriented use of both sets of books.

Stories of benefits that have come to people who tithe flash on the pages of history. God's people have learned that when they tithe, they thrive. But no matter how many spectacular accounts we can cite of how God provided for people's needs when they tithed, our personal motive for tithing must be to show love for God and to obey what He has said so clearly in the Bible.

One-third of Jesus' parables deal with money and possessions. One-sixth of the entire New Testament teachings have to do with money and the grateful use of the possessions God has entrusted to us.

Money is an extension of ourselves—our time, skill, labor, our personality and achievements reduced to negotiable form. To the extent we give God our money, we give Him that which represents ourselves.

It is possible to give our money without giving ourselves, but we cannot really give ourselves to the Lord without giving our money. And the tithe is the biblical plan of where we begin giving. Actually, tithing is not giving. That tenth is God's already. Real giving begins after we turn back to God the tenth that is His. It was never ours in the first place. And we give the tenth back to Him because God has commanded it; and because of His love in Christ, we do it out of an overflowing heart of praise and thanksgiving.

Malachi 3:7-10 is in force for Christians as much as it was when the Lord spoke it to His people. " 'Return to Me, and I will return to you,' says the Lord of hosts. 'But you said, 'In what way shall we return?' 'Will a man rob God? Yet you have robbed Me!' But you say, 'In what way have we robbed You?' 'In tithes and offerings. You are cursed with a curse, for you have robbed Me, even this whole nation. Bring all the tithes into the storehouse, that there may be food in My house, and prove Me now in this,' says the Lord of hosts, 'If I will not open for you the windows of heaven and pour out for you such blessing that there will not be room enough to receive it.' "

That challenge, warning, and obligation is the irreducible mandate for all Christians who would seek to be free. We cannot be free and rob God! Using the first tenth for other than the Lord's work is spiritual embezzlement.

I think the tithe is meant to be used for the work of the local church and Christian causes. Giving, according to the Scriptures, comes after the tithes are paid. In ancient biblical times the tithe was paid for the work of the priests of God and for the worship of the Temple. In the New Testament, they were given for spreading the gospel and for human suffering and need.

Today our tithes are given to God for His mission and evangelism through the local church. We belong to the Lord and to one another in the body of Christ, the church. Christ has called us together and entrusts to us the spiritual gifts and material resources to accomplish His work. To be a "member" means that each of us is a part of the body. Our tithes belong primarily to the church where we are fed spiritually and through which we reach out in love to the world through our evangelism and missions.

It is my opinion that there can be no continuing freedom in Christ if we receive the blessings of our spiritual family in Christ without gratitude-giving. "Christ loved the church and gave Himself for it" is the motive of our tithes and offerings to the work of the church. He calls us to love Him and to love His church. Thus, we respond in our giving not just to the needs of the budget, but to Christ Himself and the biblical mandate of the tithe.

The point is that we can't outgive the Lord. He has elected to do His work through His people. When we become agents of His blessing to others and His kingdom comes, He can make us partners in the adventure of giving. Then we are ready for the exciting fourth step to financial freedom. Once gratitude is our attitude and the tithe is our basic guide, we begin to discover the amazing secret of giving. The Lord entrusts additional resources for us to give for needs He puts on our hearts.

Step 4. Yield control of your checkbook to God's direction. Your checkbook can become a channel of God's special provision for particular needs. This is one of the most adventuresome aspects of giving I've discovered in recent years. The idea is that after our tithes are paid, the Lord brings to our attention concerns and calls us into prayer to receive His guidance about what we are to expect that He will provide for us to give. Our task in response is to make a faith promise of an amount He puts on our hearts. Then we are to wait expectantly for the additional income He entrusts to us. When it is received, our responsibility is simply to deposit it in our checking account and then write a check for the need for which He gave it to us.

This is how it works for me. I keep a tithing account to tabulate my stewardship. A tenth of all income belongs to the Lord. When that is paid consistently, I'm able to share in the Lord's delight in giving me unexpected, additional resources for specific opportunities. Each one is prayed over carefully. When an inner signal of rightness is given by the Lord, I ask for clear guidance of an amount I should trust Him to provide for me to give. It's worked repeatedly. Often, the exact amount I felt led to commit as a faith promise comes in from an unexpected source and is passed on to the purpose for which the Lord gave it to me.

Many people in my congregation are sharing this adventure with me. For example, each year we have a special Missions Sunday. In addition to mission work covered through the church budget, we outline special needs around the world. Each member is free to select one, seek the Lord's guidance for an amount to commit in a faith promise, and then to wait patiently for the Lord's added blessing to be able to pay it in the following months.

The astonishing thing is the way the Lord does provide. Unexpected money comes in from unanticipated sources. Tax rebates, inheritances, bonuses from work, payments of debts that people had owed for years and had been written off, and gifts received from unplanned sources—all are signs of the Lord's specific answers so we can pay our faith promises.

This has a faith-building residual that sets us free. We realize again that the Lord knows not only our needs, but the needs of the world. He wants to use us if we will cooperate. Suddenly money becomes a powerful commodity for blessing, and not just a false image of our worth.

Step 5. Lay up for yourself treasures in heaven. Jesus said, "Do not lay up for yourselves treasures on earth, where moth and rust destroy and where thieves break in and steal; but lay up for yourselves treasures in heaven, where neither moth nor rust destroys and where thieves do not break in and steal. For where your treasure is, there your heart will be also" (Matthew 6:19-21).

I've pondered that challenge a lot. How do you get a treasure into heaven? The answer is found in response to another question. Who is going to heaven? We are. In Greek, the word treasure is used not for the valued object but for the container. When Jesus challenges us to lay up treasures in heaven, He's really telling us to use money and the things we possess with it in a way that makes us, His treasure, ready for heaven. It's as if He said, "Your heart is the treasure. You are destined to live forever. Now prepare your treasure in a way that's fit for heaven." How we use money often determines who is lord on the throne of our hearts. Some of us will be very uncomfortable in heaven if our passion in this life has been money. The heart container, our treasure, will be unprepared to enjoy the Lord.

But press the point further. Who else goes to heaven? Other people. Therefore, the only other way to lay up treasure in heaven is to help others get there. That provides an excellent basis for determining the priorities of the kinds of causes to which we pay our tithes and give our gifts. People should be the focus.

Will the funds we give be used to introduce people to the Savior, help them to grow in Him, care for their physical needs, and heal aching sores in society? Often caring for people's temporal needs gives us an opportunity to meet their spiritual needs. Evangelism, mission, and practical programs to alleviate suffering become the priorities. And any church is worthy of receiving our tithes and gifts only if these are primary goals.

Imagine the joy of entering heaven and being greeted by the people who are there because you personally introduced them to Christ or were the Lord's channel of providing the resources for workers and programs which did. Your treasure will be those waiting for you. And your own heart, prepared and liberated by generosity will be able to enjoy fully the spiritual delight of the company of heaven.

These five steps are a sure cure for philarguria. The love of money is healed only by a greater love. When we love the Lord above all else, money can be a tangible tender of our thanksgiving.

Put your hand out in front of you. Your five fingers on that hand provide a guide for our fivefold inventory. Touch each finger as you answer these questions.

- Have you accepted that the Lord owns all you have and are?
- Have you responded with an attitude of gratitude?
- Have you faithfully tithed all He's given you the strength to earn?
- Are you willing to enter the adventure of giving beyond the tithe as the Lord provides?
- And has the way you've used money prepared your heart to be your treasure in heaven along

with others you've helped get there?

If you've said "Yes!" to all five, now place your hand in the Lord's hand. You are His partner, steward, and liberated adventurer.

9

The Freedom To Know, Be, Enjoy, & Express Yourself

Chapter Nine

The Freedom To Know, Be, Enjoy, and Express Yourself

Now we come to the essence of the essence of freedom in the Spirit. The center of the center of the truth about what it means to be a liberated person. And at that center is a powerful paradox. It is the secret of being free to know ourselves, be ourselves, enjoy ourselves, and express ourselves.

Who Are You?

So often we are told, "Just be yourself!" Just? The advice is given as if it were easy to be ourselves. How can you be yourself if you don't really know who you are?

There are so many pressures on us to conform or shape our lives into the molds of society's ideas of success and happiness. Often we are pulled in many

153

different directions by family, friends, people at work, even fellow Christians. They use powerful manipulative devices to cram us into those molds, such as solicitous affirmation when we acquiesce or withdrawal of approval and love when we get out of line. Some of us give in to the pressure; others of us rebel. Giving in often causes inner anger, and rebellion can lead to eccentric behavior just to prove we won't be controlled.

The theme song of much of our culture is "I've Got To Be Me!" But once we've asserted our right to be ourselves, we're faced with the demanding responsibility of deciding who we are. Actually who we are is a composite of what we think is important, the kind of personality we project, the goals we are determined to achieve, and the values we maintain.

But often the "I've got to be me!" is a whistling-in-the-dark assertion, exposing that we don't know who the "me" is. If we did know, we wouldn't need to protest so vociferously our right to be ourselves. And all too often the concentration on being ourselves leads us away from our potential. We are so busy defending ourselves there's no time or energy left to discover and be who we really are.

A strange mystery of life is that the more we concentrate on realizing ourselves, the less we are the unique persons God destined us to be. Meanwhile our freedom is lost fighting off people pressures and defensive self-assertion.

The undeniable truth is that the self is a reflection of the influence of models we admire, personalities we want to emulate, and the picture of ourselves we have projected on the video screen of our imagination. The important question is: Does that picture, painted with the varied colors and shadings of all that has shaped our self-image represent the fully developed self the Lord created us to be?

And so we stand at the crossroads. It is crucial to see the very different destinations of both roads: self-assertion and self-surrender. The destination of self-assertion is achievement of our purposes, plans, professional goals, and personality structure. The other road is the way of self-surrender to the Lord's purposes and plans for us and its destination is the transformation of our personality into His image. The first road ends in self-centeredness, the second in true self-realization.

The reason so many Christians are not free is that they are trying to travel both roads at the same time. Or what's worse, they are determined to get the Lord to help them become what they want to be. Now the words of the song change: "I've got to be me—and Lord, I expect You to give me the strength and courage to pull it off!"

Recently, at a meeting of pastors, the conversation drifted into a discouraging discussion of difficult people whose personality patterns, attitudes, and ways of relating to others was crippling their effectiveness as Christians. The conclusion was, "Well, that's the way things have always been. Their personalities are set in concrete. The chances of them changing are remote."

Is that true? I'm afraid it is—unless they experience Christ's secret of the transformation of personality. They will not be free and they will rob the people around them of their freedom until they discover and live the powerful paradox of being Christ's free person.

The Powerful Paradox

Here it is in two challenging dimensions: Either

deny yourself or be denied your unique self; either lose your life or you will lose the possibility of all your life was meant to be. Jesus stated the paradox pointedly: "... If anyone desires to come after Me, let him deny himself, and take up his cross daily, and follow Me. For whoever desires to save his life will lose it, but whoever loses his life for My sake will save it. For what advantage is it to a man if he gains the whole world, and is himself destroyed or lost?" (Luke 9:23-25).

Familiarity with these words from the New Testament can blunt their liberating power. At first Jesus' challenge sounds negative. But on further reflection, we discover that He has given us the profound secret of lasting freedom in *knowing, being, enjoying,* and *expressing* our true selves. Let's consider all four as we open the great treasure of the spiritual and psychological truth Jesus gave to set us free.

Know Yourself

To know yourself is to deny yourself. But how can the denial of self lead to understanding of the self? At the core of the seemingly negative idea is a very positive possibility. Jesus is calling for the denial of a lesser self for the freeing of greater self. We give up self-interest, self-determination, self-aggrandizement, and self-defensiveness. The goal is not the protection of ourselves but the achievement of a much more creative picture of ourselves.

The denial of self is not the foolish idea of getting rid of self. That can't be done. The self is the container and transmitter of our thoughts, desires, personality, and vision. We can't obliterate self-awareness any more than we can stop breathing. What we can do is open ourselves to Christ's searching and penetrating honesty. When we deny ourselves, we deny our privacy and right to control the development of ourselves. Self-denial is lowering the drawbridge of our castled self-determinism. It's inviting Christ, the surgeon of the soul, to diagnose who we are and perform surgery on our thinking, attitudes, and personality, cutting away all that interferes with us being liberated people.

Then the Lord gives us a new past and a new future. The key is to take up our cross daily and follow Him. Luke alone among the gospel writers uses the word "daily" indicating the persistent, evolving, ongoing process. Paul exposes the meaning. "I have been crucified with Christ; it is no longer I who live, but Christ lives in me; and the life which I now live in the flesh I live by faith in the Son of God, who loved me and gave Himself for me" (Galatians 2:20). He also said, "I die daily" (1 Corinthians 15:31). To take up our crosses daily is to crucify our self-assertiveness on a daily basis. The death and resurrection cycle is repeated each day as we surrender our lives to the Lord and are raised by His power to new levels of life.

Taking up our cross daily, dying to self each day, is the secret of enjoying freedom in Christ to the fullest every day. If we commit our needs to Him today, He not only releases us from the strain and stress of running our own lives, but He takes care of our tomorrows. Often obedience today makes it possible for Him to bless us with what He has prepared for a future day. That was illustrated vividly in the life of Eric Liddell in the movie *Chariots of Fire*.

At the Paris Olympics in 1924, the Christian athlete denied himself the right to participate in running on Sunday. He held firm beliefs about observing the

Sabbath. He would not contradict his convictions and refused to run the race for which he had spent years of arduous preparation. Later in the week, because of the magnanimity of a friend and the intervention of the Lord in arranging the circumstances, Liddell was given the opportunity to enter another race. In that event he won the gold medal, placing first in the race. What he denied himself one day because of obedience to the Lord was given Him on another day. And Liddell gave the Lord the glory for his victory. The same denial of self marked the athlete's life in his subsequent missionary ministry and his stirring witness to Christ in a Japanese concentration camp during World War II.

The death of self-control is the secret of Christ-control. The old self, centered in on its selfish desires, limited goals, and voracious need for success and advancement is progressively replaced with a new self remolded in Christ's image. We become the model of our admiration. If our self-image must be defended at all costs, we will remain the person we are. If, on the other hand, Christ is invited to live in us and given full access to our thinking, willing, and emotional responses, we will become more like Him every day.

Dr. F.B. Meyer described an experience in his life which helps us discover how to do that. When he was a young man he was very irritable. An old man told him a secret of overcoming that proclivity. The man had found freedom from irritability by turning to the Lord the moment he felt it coming on and saying, "Thy sweetness, Lord."

Amy Carmichael comments on Dr. Meyer's discovery in a very helpful way. "Take the opposite of your temptation and look up inwardly, naming the

opposite; Untruth—Thy truth, Lord; Unkindness—
Thy kindness, Lord; Impatience—Thy patience,
Lord; Selfishness—Thy unselfishness, Lord; Rough-
ness—Thy gentleness, Lord; Discourtesy—Thy cour-
tesy, Lord; Resentment, inward heat, fuss—Thy
sweetness, Lord, Thy calmness, Thy peacefulness.
I think that no one who tries this very simple plan
will ever give it up. It takes for granted, of course,
that all is yielded—the "I" dethroned.[1]

Responding to the opportunity to follow Christ is
to adopt His purposes as our purposes. We discover
the joy of serving rather than being served. Focusing on the self shrivels the growth of the self. Center-
ing our attention on Christ and the people He puts
in our lives develops the self into a composite of new
characteristics: love, forgiveness, compassion, and
sacrificial service. Our attitudes change. We are not
enervated by constant efforts to defend our turf. We
are freed from aggressive competition, jealousy, and
envious hostility. We become much less sensitive to
what people do to us and far more sensitive to their
needs and what the Lord wants to do for them.

To know ourselves requires the eyes of Christ. He
sees us both as we are and what we can be by His
indwelling power. He gives us the courage to change
aspects of the riverbed of self which block the flow
of His Spirit in and through us. But then He shows
us how we would look, act, react, and perform with
our talents multiplied by His gifts of love, wisdom,
discernment, daring faith, and courageous vision.

When we seek to know ourselves with self-analysis

[1] Amy Carmichael, *Edges of His Ways* (Christian Literature
Crusade, Fort Washington, PA, 1975), p. 100.

apart from Christ we end up not really knowing ourselves. Our minds play tricks on us. They block out ruthless honesty where it is needed and positive affirmation where it is required. The self eludes analysis of the self. But the more we know of Christ the more we can deal with what we've been and the more we can dare to be the unique miracle He wants to work in us to produce.

Be Yourself

Jesus goes on to tell us the next part of His secret of personal freedom: **To be yourself, lose yourself.** "For whoever desires to save his life will lose it, but whoever loses his life for My sake will save it." There are two key words for life used in the New Testament. *Psuchē* is used for natural life, the perishing and limited physical existence of a person and transitory affairs, possessions, and relationships. *Zoē* is a nobler word for the quality of spiritual life offered to us in a relationship with the Lord and as recipients of His Spirit in us. The word *psuchē* is used here in Jesus' admonition. Relinquishing our control of our physical, emotional, and relational life makes it possible for us to receive the abundant and eternal life Christ came and comes to offer us.

To lose, *apolesei*, from *apollumi*, is a term borrowed from the world of commerce. Something which was our possession is traded for something else. What we gave up is no longer ours. But in the context of the passage we are considering, what we gain is infinitely more valuable. The exchange of *psuchē* for *zoē* is dramatized in John, Chapter 10. Jesus says, "... I have come that they may have life, and that they may have it more abundantly. I am the good shepherd. The good shepherd gives His life for the sheep" (John 10:10,11).

The life, *psuchē,* He gave on Calvary was to give abundant life, *zoē.* The life of God revealed incarnate in Jesus Christ was imparted to all who would receive because of the atonement of Jesus' physical life as the Lamb of God. The resurrection was God's triumphant validation of that sacrificial death. The love revealed melts our ironclad grip on our *psuchē.* Now Christ is alive to impart *zoē* to us. Abundant life is the constant flow of His presence around, in, and through us.

The self filled with Christ's *zoē* produces a new person in our physical bodies. That person is alive forever, death has no power over us, and we are free to live with abandoned joy during the days of the brief span of our existence on earth. We know who we are because we know Whose we are. And we can be the person He enables us to be because of His life in us. Fear of being ourselves is gone. Our new self is a manifestation of the reigning Christ. Arrogant or defensive self-confidence is replaced by a winsome and contagious Christ-confidence.

Jim Elliot, the martyred missionary, once said, "He is no fool who gives what he cannot keep to gain what he cannot lose." That's our confidence. A life surrendered to Christ becomes His post-resurrection home. Our security is not in our adequacy, but in His unlimited power surging through us, changing our personalities, and guiding us in daring expression of the loved, forgiven, transformed person He is enabling us to be. John Henry Newman said, "Fear not that your life will come to an end, but rather that it shall never have a beginning." But the invasion of Christ's *zoē* into our *psuchē* gives us a beginning of true life that nothing can destroy.

One of the most significant results is that we are

free from the pressures to be anything other than the new creation Christ is producing in us. Doing His will becomes the joy of our lives. We are not distressed in life's decisions because we can depend on His guidance.

God does reveal what we are to be and do in each relationship and situation. We can dare to attempt what others would consider impossible because of His unlimited strength surging in and through us. We don't have to be crippled by what we've been, or constricted by our previously negative idea of what is possible. Being ourselves is letting Christ shine through us!

Enjoy Yourself

It is as you open your life to Christ that you become able to truly enjoy yourself—the new Christ-centered self. *To enjoy yourself, allow Christ to enjoy you.*

I am convinced that people who enjoy themselves are those who know the delicious feeling of being enjoyed. A friend of mine is a fun-loving, unselfconscious person who enjoys being the unique miracle the Lord is producing in him. He spreads that contagious delight to others around him. His ministry of encouragement never seems to bog down in self-condemnation issuing in negativism. He's not the person he used to be and he's not yet all that the Lord has planned for him to be. But he is a joyful person, free to enjoy himself.

Often, our enjoyment of ourselves is debilitated because we don't like the way we look, or by lack of self-affirmation because of physical limitations. We dislike ourselves because we are too tall or too short, or have some disability which makes us think of ourselves as unattractive. Reading between the lines of Paul's writings, we sense that he was not a first-century Charlton Heston. And yet he could say, "But we have this treasure in earthen vessels, that the excellence of the power may be of God and not of us" (2 Corinthians 4:7). The treasure of Christ's Spirit in the apostle was more important than the vessel.

The other day, I visited a fellow pastor who is one of our nation's most able communicators. He has a receding hairline. I seldom notice because of the radiance of his face. On the wall next to the mirror in a private restroom attached to his office is an embroidered plaque. On it are these words: "God made a few perfect heads. Others He covered with hair." There's a man who can enjoy himself coupling a look in the mirror with a laugh at himself.

I am constantly amazed at how few people enjoy themselves. Their freedom to know and be themselves is frustrated by the earthen vessel rather than the power of the Lord which it can contain. The result is that we become more concerned about how we look or come across to others than allowing Christ to shine through the vessel.

The same thing can happen to us because of our remorse over mistakes and failures. "How can the Lord love and use a person who did or said that?" we demand of ourselves in self-incrimination. But He does. None of us is perfect. Good thing. Our pride over our self-generated purity would make us unusable. The Lord delights in surprising the world around us with what He can do with imperfect people like us.

When we acknowledge that, we can give the Lord the glory. Our enjoyment of being used in spite of our limitations will spill over to other people. The task of the local congregation is not to convince people of how bad they are, but how powerful God is.

A conversation with a friend drifted into concern about a mutual friend. He is a very gifted man who is plagued with lack of self-esteem. My friend said, "I wish that guy enjoyed himself more!" My response was, "Perhaps the place for us to begin to help him is to tell him how much we enjoy him. There's a lot about him I do enjoy." After that conversation I thought long and hard about the people in my life who need to know that I enjoy them. I decided to tell them so—to express my feelings so they would know.

Express Yourself

Finally, when we know who we are, dare to be ourselves, and enjoy the unique miracle each of us is, *we are free to express ourselves.* Under the Lord's guidance we can set our priorities and goals, arrange our lives on His agenda, and do what He has led us to desire for our lives. We don't have to be victims of people or circumstances. Even those situations that seem like limitations to our free self-expression can, by His grace and power, be turned into opportunities to communicate the real person inside us He is enabling us to be. That freedom is spelled out in the dynamics of honesty, directness, and genuineness.

By honesty, I mean the freedom to allow other people to know us. Being honest is the opposite of pretense and posturing. Honesty is vulnerability. The Lord loves us as we are, but has not chosen to leave us as we are. Therefore, we are people in transition. The best of what we are to become is still to be. We are free to admit our shortcomings and problems. No one has it all together. So why should we pretend we have? There is a relaxed, winsome freedom about honest people. They are open about their failures and as a result fail less. The tight spring of self-generated perfectionism has been unwound. They are free to make life a continuous series of new beginnings.

That enables directness. We can state what we believe and want from life because our convictions have been shaped by time with the Lord in prayer, reflection on our goals by reading the Bible, and a deep commitment of our wills to seek and do the Lord's will. Since our self-esteem is no longer dominated by people's vacillating opinions or manipulative criticism, we don't have to do an equivocating "duty dance" to be liked. People who spend their energies trying to be liked usually don't like themselves. In Christ, we are more than liked, we are loved profoundly.

And that quality of acceptance and cherishing esteem frees us to be genuine. Real, authentic. People will begin to appreciate the consistency. When they discover that integrity in us, rooted in Christ, they will relate with greater directness with us. They will not have to squander precious energy worrying about what we really mean or desire. Most of all, they will never have to wonder about our love for them. Christ's love in us will become the consistent, reliable basis of our attitudes toward them.

Being this kind of free person may seem like an impossibility. Each one of us knows how far he is from that quality of freedom. Admitting that is the first step. And that brings us back to where we began this book. *Think freedom. Think clearly about your freedom in Christ, His atonement, righteousness in Him, the power of His indwelling Spirit, and His absolutely reliable strength for all of life.*

Feelings follow thought. Think freedom in Christ, and then feel freely, forgive freely, act freely, receive freely, and dream freely. Remembering always, "Now the Lord is the Spirit, and where the Spirit of the Lord is, there is freedom" (2 Corinthians 3:17, NIV).

10

Freedom
At 5,000 Feet

Chapter Ten

Freedom At 5,000 Feet

I boarded a United Airlines flight at Kansas City bound for Los Angeles. The previous two days had been an exhausting round of speeches and meetings. I settled into my seat, leaned my head back and fell asleep just as the plane took off. I slept soundly for about an hour when I was awakened by the pilot's urgent voice over the intercom.

"Ladies and gentlemen, we will not be going directly to Los Angeles. Instead, we will be landing in Denver, changing planes, and then we will proceed on to our destination. No explanation can be made at this point. You will be given a full report as soon as we are on the ground in Denver."

A rumble of concern passed through the airplane. Flight attendants exchanged troubled glances. Passengers expressed a combination of consternation over the delay this would cause and fear over what might be causing what was obviously an emergency landing. Was there something wrong with the plane? Impassable weather ahead? We didn't know, and the pilot wasn't telling.

As soon as we landed on the runway in Denver, the pilot stopped the plane and spoke to the passengers anxiously awaiting word. "This is your pilot again, ladies and gentlemen. Allow me to explain why we have detoured our flight plan and landed here in Denver. After we took off from Kansas City we were radioed by Central Control and told that a phone call had been received informing us that a bomb had been placed on board this flight. It was set to go off at 5,000 feet in our descent into Los Angeles. Now, the officials of United Airlines have done some quick figuring. Denver is 5,280 feet high, 280 feet above the bomb's detonation and explosion point. We will evacuate the plane immediately and all luggage and carry-on bags will be searched thoroughly. Thank you for your cooperation. Please remain calm; and sorry for the delay."

At this point police cars, fire engines, and television trucks zoomed up and stopped at safe distance in case of an explosion of the aircraft.

All the passengers were evacuated and taken by bus to the terminal. In the long wait for new equipment to be serviced and brought around to the gate, people from the flight milled around quietly. Some made hurried calls on the pay phones nearby. There was no excited chatter about what might have happened if the airline officials had not been quick enough to work out the ingenious plan to land higher than the bomb's detonation point. Everyone seemed preoccupied with thoughts of their near-encounter with death.

When we boarded the new plane for Los Angeles at long last, I asked a flight attendant if the bomb had been found or if it was a false alarm. She said she didn't know and feared it might have been so well hidden that it might have been reloaded on this new plane with the transfer of the luggage.

I doubted that, and yet, the possibility lingered with unsettling, growing persistence in my mind during the time of the flight from Denver to Los Angeles. What if it were true? What if the bomb exploded at 5,000 feet on our descent into Los Angeles? How did I feel if this were my last day of physical life? Was I ready? Was I sure where I would spend eternity?

A deep assurance flooded me. I belonged to the Lord, live or die. I was ready for heaven whenever it began, that day or forty years from then. I began to pray prayers of thanksgiving for the goodness of the Lord through the years of my life. My loved ones passed before my mind's eye. I praised the Lord for each one and all he or she meant to me.

Then my mind drifted back across the years. I laughed and cried inside as I remembered all I'd been through. The Lord had been faithful. He had called me and used me. All the glory belonged to Him. I pictured congregations I'd served, people I'd been privileged to introduce to the Lord, and some difficult people who had contributed to my growth in patience and endurance. Memories of childhood, loyal friends through the years, and memorable times in my beloved Scotland as a student and subsequently many happy summers of study there—all paraded before the inner vision of my memory. I had been blessed beyond measure, more than any person could expect in a dozen lifetimes. And I knew I had nothing to fear if the plane exploded. What more

could I ask of the Lord than He had given already—
except, that I spend eternity with Him?

I felt truly free. All the concerns on my mind when
I boarded the plane in Kansas City shriveled into in-
significant proportion—the size they should have
been anyway. The heavy work load I was carrying
with my church and a national television ministry
seemed lightened and took on new excitement. Any
worries tucked in the corner of my mind draining
off precious energy were brought to the forefront of
my thinking and dismissed as inconsequential in the
light of the fact that this might be the last day of the
earthly portion of my eternal life.

Then I thought of this book that I was in the process of writing at the time. It might never be finished,
I thought. I wondered if people would find what was
written and publish it posthumously. Of one thing
I was sure without any doubt: I believed what I had
written and was more convinced than ever by this
experience that the precious gift of freedom was indeed my rebirth-right.

The pilot's voice interrupted my prayers of praise
and thanksgiving. "Ladies and gentlemen, we've
been on our descent flight plan into Los Angeles. We
have just cleared 5,000 feet and are proceeding to
land safely. Thank you for your patience, and God
bless you!"

He had. I joined the other passengers in applaud-
ing and cheering. As we taxied to the Los Angeles
United Airlines terminal, I whispered a prayer,
"Lord, thank You for allowing me to go through
this experience. It has given me assurance and
renewed courage for whatever You have ahead for
me in the future. I have nothing to fear. Any fear
of death is behind me. Now I know with absolute

confidence that I am released to live with unfettered freedom!"

As I left the airplane, the flight attendant winked and said, "Thank you for flying with United. This has been just another uneventful day in the life of the 'A' team!" I smiled and said, "Yes, but this 'A' team has a super Coach!" pointing up with my fore-finger. The young woman's face became intent. "I've been watching you throughout both legs of this worrisome flight. You're a Christian, aren't you? So am I! Isn't it great to be free of fear?" I agreed, shook her hand, and left the aircraft.

As I walked through the terminal, Paul's words in 2 Corinthians 3:17,18 kept surging through my mind, over and over again. "Now the Lord is the Spirit; and where the Spirit of the Lord is, there is liberty. But we all, with unveiled face, beholding as in a mirror the glory of the Lord, are being transformed into the same image from glory to glory, just as by the Spirit of the Lord."

Where the Spirit of the Lord is, there is liberty. Indeed! I had known that before, but knew it in a fresh way as that day ended. And the Lord is wherever we are in life's routine or breathtaking excitement. He's in homes, hospital rooms, factories, offices, executive suites, in a farmer's barn, at a laborer's bench, and a scholar's library.

He is our omnipresent, ubiquitous Lord of all life. And wherever He is, He's ready to give love, forgiveness, righteousness, and the composite experiential gift of them all—freedom!

So don't resist; whatever happens, the Spirit of the Lord will be there.

He is Jehovah-Shammah, "the Lord is there."

He is Immanuel, "God with us."

He is our triumphant Savior, offering us righteousness through His atonement.

He is indwelling Lord with abiding power.

And He is the Spirit who sets us free!

Other Books by Lloyd John Ogilvie:

A Life Full of Surprises	Abingdon Press
Ask Him Anything	Word Books
Autobiography of God	Regal Books
Congratulations—God Believes in You!	Word Books
Cup of Wonder	Tyndale House
Drumbeat of Love	Word Books
God's Best For My Life	Harvest House
God's Will For Your Life	Harvest House
If I Should Wake Before I Die	Regal Books
Let God Love You	Word Books
Life As It Was Meant To Be	Regal Books
Life Without Limits	Word Books
Loved and Forgiven	Regal Books
Lord of the Ups and Downs	Regal Books
Radiance of the Inner Splendor	Upper Room
The Beauty of Caring	Harvest House
The Beauty of Friendship	Harvest House
The Beauty of Love	Harvest House
The Beauty of Sharing	Harvest House
The Bush Is Still Burning	Word Books
When God First Thought of You	Word Books
You've Got Charisma	Abingdon Books